Michael & Sue Price

Internet
For Seniors

For the Over 50s

In easy steps is an imprint of Computer Step
Southfield Road · Southam
Warwickshire CV47 0FB · United Kingdom
www.ineasysteps.com

Notice of Liability

Every effort has been made to ensure that this book
contains accurate and current information. However,
Computer Step and the author shall not be liable for
any loss or damage suffered by readers as a result of
any information contained herein.

Trademarks

All trademarks are acknowledged as belonging to their
respective companies.

Printed and bound in the United Kingdom

ISBN-13 978-1-84078-318-6
ISBN-10 1-84078-318-4

Contents

1 Get Started

This chapter outlines the Internet and the World Wide Web, discusses the facilities you need to get on the Internet from your computer, and introduces the latest version of Internet Explorer, that gives you safe and secure access to the Internet.

The Internet

The Internet (**Inter**connected **Net**work) is a global network connecting millions of computers, organized in thousands of commercial, academic, domestic and government networks and located in over 100 countries. The Internet is sometimes called the Information Highway, because it provides the transportation and routing for the information exchanged between the connected computers.

The computers on the Internet are connected by a variety of methods, including the telephone system, wired networks, wireless (radio) networks, cable TV and even satellite.

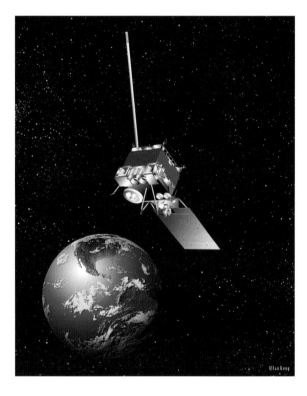

Some sections are commercial, others are academic or government, and no single organization owns the Internet as a whole. It is simply made up of the individual, independent networks and computers, whose owners and operators decide which Internet methods to use and which local services to offer to the global Internet community.

Internet services

The services offered could include one or more of:

- Electronic mail (email)

  This allows you and other Internet users to send and receive messages.

- FTP (File Transfer Protocol)

  This allows your computer to retrieve files from a remote computer and view or save them on your computer.

- Internet Service Providers (ISPs)

  These, as the name suggests, provide points of access to the Internet. You need an ISP account, plus the means of connecting your computer to one of their computers.

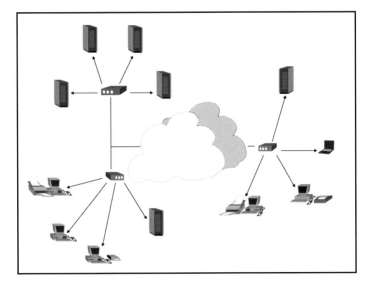

- **World Wide Web (WWW)**

  Also known as the **Web,** this is made up of collections of files and documents that may include images, animation, video and hyperlinks to other documents. These can be on the same computer, or on different computers, anywhere on the Internet.

Don't forget

There are other ways to connect to the Internet that don't require a computer, such as cell phone, or a PDA device.

Don't forget

A location on the Web is known as a website. It will have a home page, the document that you see when you enter the site. It might have additional documents (web pages) and files, usually related to the main theme or focus.

Hot tip

To visit a website and follow the hyperlinks in the web pages you will need an Internet browser (see page 14).

6

Requirements

To connect to the Internet, there are a number of things that you'll require:

 A computer equipped for use on the Internet. In this book we assume that you are using a Windows-based PC (see page 11).

 A means of connecting your PC (or PCs) to the computers at your ISP, including the hardware components, the communications software and the cabling or phone links.

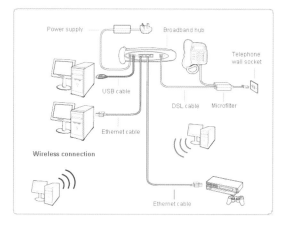

 An ISP account that will provide access to the Internet. You may also need email services, which would normally use the same account.

 Appropriate software on your computer, to exchange information with other computers on the Internet, and to send and receive emails.

We'll look at each of these in turn, so you know all the tasks that are involved in setting up your computer, and can identify what remains to be done.

Internet enabled computer

If you purchased your computer within the last three or four years it will almost certainly be adequate for most activities on the Internet. If you have an older computer, review these hardware and software specifications to see if it will meet your needs for Internet access.

Processor
If your computer has a Pentium 500MHz processor or anything faster than this, you won't be restricted by the power of your computer.

Operating System
While any version of Windows will allow you to access the Internet, for the best security you should consider upgrading to a current or recent version, e.g. Windows Vista or Windows XP.

Memory
Although it is possible to run your computer with less memory, your use of the Internet will be smoother and more effective if you have memory of 256MB or more installed.

Hard Disk Drive
Check the free space on your hard drive. If there is 10GB or more available, you'll have no problems with disk space. Any less, and you might wish to consider replacing the drive, or simply adding a second drive.

Display Monitor and Adapter
To take full advantage of the Internet, you should preferably have a monitor 17" or larger, capable of displaying Hicolor (16bit), Trucolor (24bit) or better, at a resolution of 1024 x 768 pixels. CRT monitors and flat screen LCD displays are equally suitable, though the latter are much easier to house.

Don't forget

Other requirements include a soundcard, speakers and DVD drive, if you want to play videos on your computer. You may also want a printer and perhaps a scanner, but these are not essentials for accessing the Internet.

Hot tip

To check the specifications for your computer, open the Control Panel and locate the entry for System. Double-click this to see the operating system level, the processor type and the memory installed.

Don't forget

Open My Computer (XP) or Computer (Vista), select the individual drive and check the size and the space available on the drive, displayed in the Details panel on the left of the window.

Connection types

The type of connection you need depends on how much use you will be making of Internet access. There are four main options, though not all are available in every region.

Dial-up

This is a low speed, low cost method for limited usage (less than say ten hours per week). It uses a Modem in your computer, which connects to a standard telephone socket. Your normal phone line is unavailable for incoming or outgoing calls while you are using the Internet.

DSL Broadband

This offers higher speed and supports a higher level of usage. It uses a DSL modem attached to your computer or alternatively a separate device known as a router. It makes use of your telephone connection, but transfers data in a digital format that allows the line to remain available for normal incoming or outgoing calls. You can if you wish leave your computer connected all the time.

You must check with your telephone company to see if DSL Broadband is available in your area.

Cable TV

If your area has Cable TV services, these may offer a broadband connection. This operates in a similar fashion to DSL Broadband, but independent of your telephone line.

Satellite

Internet via satellite services can provide you with a permanent 2-way connection to the Internet that uses no telephone line. All you need is an interface box and a small satellite dish connected to your computer.

Wireless

This is the type of connection you use with a laptop computer (or a handheld unit) when you are away from home, at an airport or hotel. Your computer has a radio modem, and the organization you are visiting provides the hub device which in turn connects to the Internet.

ISP account

Having decided the type of connection that meets your needs, you need an Internet Service Provider to complete the connection. There are several ways to identify ISPs:

- Ask friends and family which ISP they use

- Check for pre-installed links on your computer for setting up a well-known ISP, such as AOL or MSN

- Look for CDs for ISPs in the information supplied with your computer, to get onscreen instructions

- Check at your local bookstore, supermarket or computer store for ISP CDs and special offers

Windows offers a Referral Service to locate an ISP in your area. For example, in Windows XP:

1. Select Start, All Programs, Accessories, Communications to open the **New Connection Wizard**.

2. Click Next, choose **Connect to the Internet**, then click Next again.

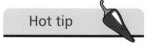
3. Select to Choose from a list of Internet Service Providers (ISPs) then click Next, pick an ISP and follow the onscreen instructions.

Internet browser software

The software used to access the Internet, once you have set up your ISP account, is the Internet Browser. For Windows this will be Internet Explorer, the version depending on which release of Windows you have on your system.

Windows XP comes with Internet Explorer 6.0 (IE6).

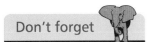

Don't forget

There are other Internet browsers, such as Firefox, Netscape and Opera. The layout may differ if you have something other than Internet Explorer, but you still should be able to take advantage of the suggestions and examples in the book.

Windows Vista uses Internet Explorer version 7.0 (IE7). This contains an improved level of security to help defend your system against malicious software. Tabs and quick tabs have been added, to make it easier for you to switch back and forth between websites. Other enhancements include advanced printing, page zooming capabilities, and support for RSS (Really Simple Syndication) feeds (see page 167).

Hot tip

IE7 protects you against the theft of personal data via fraudulent emails and fake websites, the practice known as phishing. See page 171 for details.

14

Upgrade to IE7

Internet Explorer 7 is the recommended choice for secure and convenient Internet access. However, you do not have to upgrade to Windows Vista in order to benefit from IE7. Microsoft has developed a special, stand-alone version of Internet Explorer 7.0 that runs under Windows XP with SP2. What's more, they make it available free of charge.

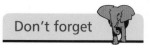

Don't forget

You need Windows XP with the SP2 (Service Pack 2) update, in order to be able to install and use this special version of IE7.

It is this combination of IE7 and Windows XP with SP2 that has been used for the illustrations in this book.

Hot tip

IE7 in Windows XP provides the same functions as in Vista, and uses the same operations and techniques, but with the older display style.

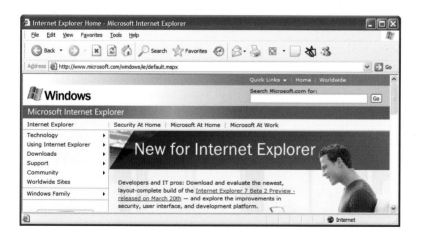

For instructions on downloading and installing the new version, go to **http://www.microsoft.com/downloads**, and search for **Internet Explorer 7**. Alternatively, call your local Microsoft office to ask for information. They may have a CD available to save you downloading the software.

Setting up

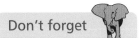

Don't forget

Generally, everything you need for accessing the Internet will already have been installed and often pre-configured for you by your computer supplier, so you can go straight on to starting your browser (see page 17).

In most cases, the instructions you require to set up and configure your Internet connection will be made available by the Internet Service Provider you have selected. However, in Windows XP the New Connection Wizard, as used for the Referral Service (see page 13) provides guidance for creating the connection. This may be useful when you are setting up, for example, a simple dial-up connection, perhaps using the ISP account from your previous computer.

1. Select Start, All Programs, Accessories, Communications and **New Connection Wizard**.

2. Click Next, choose **Connect to the Internet**, then click Next again.

Hot tip

There's usually a setup CD available from your ISP that will take you step by step through the connection process, with explanations at each stage. This will avoid setting up your connection manually.

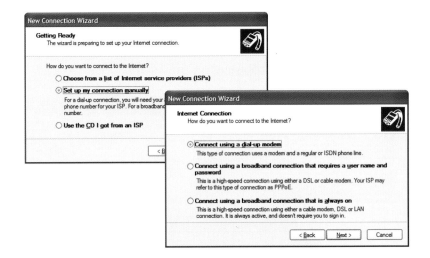

3. Select to **Set up my connection manually**, then select the type of connection (e.g. dial-up modem).

4. Provide a name and telephone number for your ISP.

5. Enter your user name and password and complete the Wizard to create the connection.

Starting Internet Explorer

The first step in browsing the Internet is to start your Internet browser software (e.g. Internet Explorer). There are two methods that you might use:

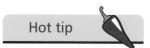

1. Select Start, and click **Internet Explorer** at the top of the list.

2. If you have the **Quick Launch bar** enabled, click its Internet Explorer icon.

In either case, the Internet Explorer application will be opened. If it is not already active, your connection to the Internet will be established. When the connection completes, the default web page is displayed.

This is known as your Home page, and you'll see the same page each time you start your browser, or whenever you press the Home button on the Command Bar. The page gets defined when your software is installed or re-configured, and is usually a news page selected by your ISP.

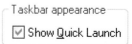

Hot tip

To enable the Quick Launch bar, right-click the Taskbar, select Properties and click the Show Quick Launch box, then click OK.

Hot tip

Default means a particular value or setting, in this case a web page, that is assigned automatically, and remains in effect until you cancel or change it.

Don't forget

You can change the defined home page to a web page that you prefer, or specify several home pages to display at the start. See page 32 for details.

Internet Explorer window

Your browser is the key component in any Internet activity so you should become familiar with all of its features.

Title bar

Address bar   Tab bar   Toolbar   Search box

Information bar

Favorites Center

Main Window

Status bar   Security Settings   Scroll bars   Zoom

Command buttons

Extra buttons

Toolbar buttons

Home   Size   Back
Feeds   Encoding   Forward
Print   Edit   Recent Pages
Page   Cut   Refresh
Tools   Copy   Stop Loading
Help   Paste   Search
              Full Screen   Options
                            Favorites Center
                            Add Favorites

2 Browse the Internet

The Internet is an enormous library of information, but it is not at all well organized, so you have to locate what you need, by name, through links or by searching, using descriptive keywords, taking full advantage of the capabilities of your browsing software.

Web page address

To find your way around the Internet, you need to understand web page addresses. For example, the sample home page (see page 17) has this web address:

http://www.virgin.net/index.html

This address is made up of several parts:

- **http://**   Indicates web pages
- **www.virgin.net**   The web server name
- **index.html**   The web page name

The web server name is itself made up of several parts:

- **www**   Indicates a host computer
- **virgin**   The company or owner name
- **net**   The type of website

There are a number of other website types that you will encounter. These include:

- **com**   Commercial website
- **org**   Organization – usually non-profit
- **ac**   Academic (e.g. university)
- **gov**   Government department

For all these web types, there are international forms, where an additional section indicates the country, for example:

- **co.uk, org.uk, ac.uk**   United Kingdom
- **com.au, org.au, edu.au**   Australia
- **co.in, org.in, ac.in**   India

Google illustrates the range of international domains supported, via their **Language Tools** link (see page 14).

(see page 17)

Don't forget

The web server name incorporates the Domain name, which consists of owner name and website type, in this case virgin.net. Other examples of domain names are:

microsoft.com

elderhostel.org

20

Beware

Individuals as well as companies can register domain names of many different types, so the name itself does not tell you anything about the owner.

Hot tip

Although there are general similarities, the naming is not entirely consistent, country to country. Some countries use co instead of com, and ac instead of edu.

Open a web page

If you find a web page address in an article or advertisement, or are given a web address by a friend, you can direct the browser to display that page. For example, to display the web page **www.pagat.com/boston/bridge.html**:

1 Start Internet Explorer (see page 17) if required, and click the address bar area. The address is highlighted.

2 Type the required web page address. This replaces the existing highlighted address.

3 Press **Enter**, or click the green arrow button, to display the required page.

(see page 17)

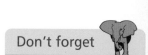

Links

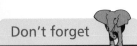

Don't forget

Hyperlinks are the fundamental element in the World Wide Web. They are also used in electronic documents such as Adobe's PDF files.

When you've displayed one web page, you can usually go on to another page without having to type a web page address. Instead, you click on items on the current page that have web addresses associated with them. These items are called Links (or Hyperlinks). They are often descriptive text, underlined and colored blue, for example.

To confirm whether a part of the page is a link:

1 Place the mouse pointer over the item. If it is a link, the pointer changes to a hand symbol, to indicate that there is a link address.

Hot tip

Sometimes, the text or graphic will change color when the mouse pointer moves over it, or it will flash, to draw your attention to the associated link.

2 The target location is shown on the status bar.

3 Sometimes, the link will be a graphic image with no distinguishing marks. Again, the mouse pointer changes to a hand symbol, to indicate a link.

4 Often, the graphic image will have a **Tool Tip** description, which appears when you place the mouse pointer over the image.

Games played with Latin suited cards

Follow links

To follow a link, left-click the associated text or graphic.

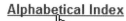

1 Click the Alphabetical Index link (see page 21). This leads to a page with links A to Z, defining sections on the same page, organized alphabetically.

2 Click the **H** link to move down the page to the location **www.pagat.com/alpha.html#h**.

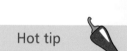

When you visit a location the color  of the link changes, typically from blue to purple, providing a visual cue that you have followed that particular link.

Address help

Internet Explorer offers you help with entering web page addresses, in several ways.

1 Click the arrow at the end of the Address bar, to see a list of web page addresses that you have typed previously, and click the one that you want.

2 If you start typing an address (as on page 20), Internet Explorer lists previously visited web pages that match the part entered so far. As soon as you see the required web page, click the entry to open it.

3 Type the company or organization name on the address bar, and then press Ctrl+Enter.

nbc

displays http://www.nbc.com/

bbc

displays http://www.bbc.co.uk/?ok

Add to Favorites

When you visit a web page that you find useful, make it easy to find another time by adding it to your list of favorites.

1 While viewing the web page, click the Add to Favorites button and select **Add to Favorites**.

2 The title of the page is suggested as the name, or you can type another perhaps more descriptive name. Click **Add** to put the page details onto the main list.

Add a Favorite

Add a Favorite
Add this webpage as a favorite. To access your favorites, visit the Favorites Center.

Name: Card Games

Create in: ☆ Favorites ⌄ [New Folder]

[Add] [Cancel]

3 Click on the **Favorites Center** button to display the list, and select any page you wish to visit.

Virgin.net ISP - Broadband Internet access

☆ Favorites | 🔊 Feeds | 🕘 History ⌄

📁 Links
📁 Microsoft
📁 Canada
📁 Crossword Tools
🖹 Card Games
🖹 Language Tools

Hot tip

Pages you visit every day can become your home pages, so they open whenever Internet Explorer opens. See page 32.

Don't forget

Press the New Folders button to create a subfolder in the Favorites list. Click the down-arrow to select a subfolder in which to store the web page details.

Hot tip

If you forgot to add a web page and you want to find it again, click the History tab in the Favorites Center, and you'll see the pages you have visited over the recent period of time.

Searching

You will find that some types of search are handled better by a particular search provider, so it is helpful to have several ready for use.

If you have no idea of the correct website, Internet Explorer will carry out a search on your behalf.

1 Click in the **Search** box to the right of the Address bar, type some keywords appropriate to the website you want, and press Enter.

kew gardens

2 Internet Explorer uses your default search engine to find web pages that are related to your search terms.

Click an entry on the list to make it your choice for the current session, or select Change Search Defaults to pick a new default, or to remove unwanted entries.

3 Scroll down or page forward as required until you find the website you want, then click the header.

4 Press the **Back** button to return to the search results.

Add search providers

If you prefer to use a different search provider, you can make additional providers available, and change the default.

1 Click the down arrow next to the search box, and select **Find More Providers**, to open the Windows Search Guide at Microsoft's website.

Hot tip

Press Ctrl+E to position the typing cursor in the Search box, without having to use the mouse.

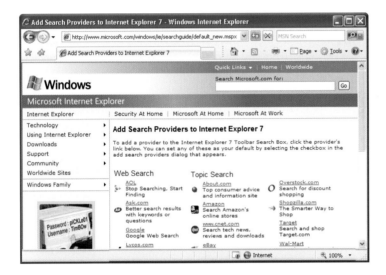

Don't forget

Internet Explorer sets the default as MSN Search, but you can add additional search providers or change the default provider.

27

2 Click the hyperlink for your preferred search provider, to display the **Add Provider** dialog.

3 Click in the box to **Make this my default search provider**, and then press **Add Provider**.

4 Select any other provider that you want to add (this time without clicking the box).

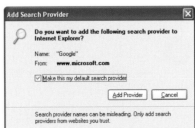

Hot tip

You can also search straight from the Address bar. Type Find or Go followed by the search words, to display the results in the current window.

Specific searches

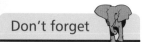

Don't forget

You can set your preferences for the language and set "mature content" filters to avoid inappropriate results.

The normal search is for pages across the Web, but there are alternatives such as local pages, groups, news, or images.

1   Type your keywords into the search box, and search using Google, to list the matching web pages.

2   Click **Images** to repeat the search, this time locating relevant images, which are displayed as thumbnails.

Hot tip

Click the image and follow the prompts to view the image full size. Right-click the image and select Save Picture As, to save a copy of it onto your hard drive.

3   Click the down arrow next to **All Image Sizes** to limit the images selected to small, medium or large sizes.

Using tabs

Tabs allow you to have more than one website open at the same time, without having to use separate windows. With web pages, links and search results on separate tabs, you switch between them using the Quick Tabs.

To open a new tab:

1. Click the **New Tab** button on the tab row or press Ctrl+T, to open a new blank page.

2. The **Quick Tabs** button is displayed, and you may also see the Welcome to Tabbed Browsing page.

3. Press the **Don't Show Again** button at the bottom of the page, and in future you'll get a blank page.

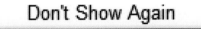

4. Type the web page location on the address bar, and the specified web page opens on the new tab.

Open new tab

Hot tip

There are several ways for you to specify a web page address, and have it open it on a new tab, as in steps 1, 2 or 3.

1 Type the web page location on the address bar, with the current tab displayed, then press **Alt+Enter**.

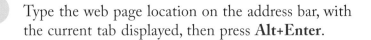

2 Right-click a hyperlink on the web page and select to **Open in New tab**.

3 Hold down the **Ctrl** key as you left-click a hyperlink on the web page.

Advanced Anagramming
Open
Open in New Tab
Open in New Window
Save Target As...
Print Target

Properties

Hot tip

If you have a three button mouse, select the hyperlink with the middle button. When you have a wheel on your mouse, that also acts as a middle button. In either case, the page opens on a new tab.

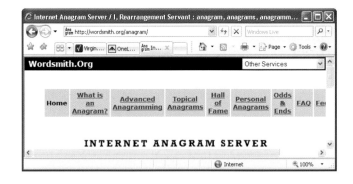

4 Click the **Quick Tabs** button to review all the tabbed pages, and select one you want.

Hot tip

Click the Tab List button next to Quick Tabs, to select from a list, or click the Scroll buttons to find a particular page on the tab row.

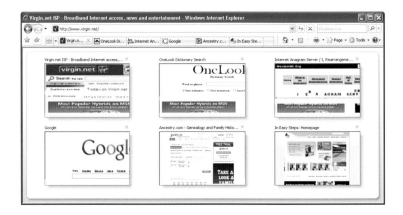

Close tabs

Having opened a number of tabs, you can close them individually or as a group.

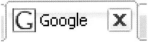

1 Click the **[X]** on an individual tab to close it, or select the tab with the center button.

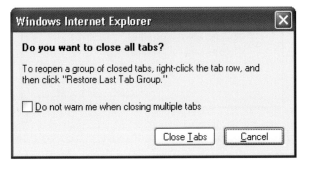

2 Right-click a tab or one of the Quick Tabs thumbnails, and select to close just that tab, or to close all the other tabs (leaving that tab open).

3 Click the **Close** button or press Alt+F4 to close Internet Explorer, and you'll be asked to confirm you want to close all the tabs.

4 The next time you open Internet Explorer, right-click the tabs row, and select **Restore Last Tab Group**. This reopens the group of tabs that were active immediately before you last closed Internet Explorer.

Don't forget

You can also close the current tab by pressing Ctrl+W. To close all the tabs except the current tab, press Ctrl+Alt+W.

Hot tip

Click the box to indicate that you do not need this reminder that there are multiple tabs open.

Hot tip

To save a group of tabs and make them available for reload, click the Add/Subscribe button and select Add Current Tabs to Favorites. You will need to provide a folder name.

Change home page

You can change the web page used as the initial page when Internet Explorer starts up.

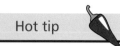
1. Open the preferred web page by typing its location on the address bar (see page 20).

2. Click the down arrow next to the Home Page button.

3. To use the current web page, select the option to Change Home Page.

4. Select the option to **Use this as your only home page**, then click Yes to apply the change.

The specified page opens automatically, when you click the Home button, or whenever you start Internet Explorer.

Blank Home Page

If you decide that you do not require a home page at all:

1. Select Remove, Remove All, and Internet Explorer will simply start on a blank page.

3 Puzzles and Solutions

Use online reference materials to look up words, get solutions to crossword clues, locate facts or resolve anagrams. You can also use the Internet as a source of entertaining puzzles and quizzes, or to locate online books, especially the classics, which you can read and research.

Solve crosswords

You might make a start by using the Internet to help you
with a crossword. Suppose you have a partially solved
crossword and want to use the Internet to help complete it.

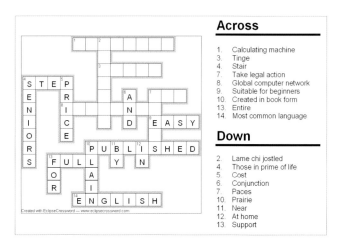

Across

1. Calculating machine
3. Tinge
4. Stair
7. Take legal action
8. Global computer network
9. Suitable for beginners
10. Created in book form
13. Entire
14. Most common language

Down

2. Lame chi jostled
4. Those in prime of life
5. Cost
6. Conjunction
7. Paces
10. Prairie
11. Near
12. At home
13. Support

34

1   Type the keywords **solve crossword** in the Search
    box and click the Search button.

2   The website at **www.oneacross.com** offers free help
    with crosswords (and anagrams and cryptograms).

Resolve clues

The OneAcross website allows you to enter complete clues, along with the number of letters required. For example:

1   Type the clue **Take legal action** and the pattern **???** (meaning three letters, all unknown), and click Go!

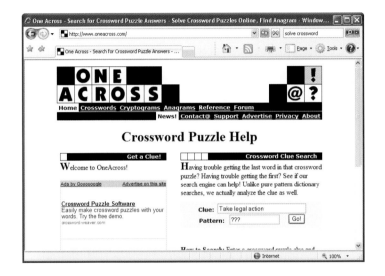

2   The website displays the answers that it finds.

Hot tip

Solve clue 7 across: Take legal action (3)

Don't forget

When you think you know one or more letters, replace the ?s in the appropriate positions by the expected letter. Use upper case if you are sure you have the correct letter, lower case otherwise.

Beware

You may get the message "We're sorry, the OneAcross server is too busy to respond at this time." Try again, or switch to another website such as OneLook (see page 37 for details).

Find anagrams

Many crosswords incorporate anagrams in the clues. The anagram server at **www.wordsmith.org** helps with these.

1. Type the anagram word or words, leaving out spaces, e.g. **lamechi** and click Get Anagrams.

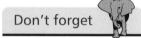

2. The website displays all the answers that it can find. These can include multiple words, abbreviations, acronyms etc.

3. For more specific answers, choose the Advanced Anagramming option.

Look up words

You can look up words in an online dictionary, for example:

1 Visit **www.onelook.com**, and type the pattern for the word, using **???**s and inserting letters you know.

2 OneLook defaults to **All Matches**, and lists the potential answers in alphabetic order.

3 Add words from the clue (separated by a colon from the word pattern). The most likely will be listed first.

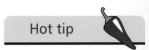

Hot tip

Solve clue 1 across: Calculating machine(8)

Don't forget

The OneLook Dictionaries website has indexed about eight million words, from around 1000 dictionaries. It finds word patterns and definitions.

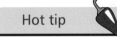

Hot tip

If there are many possibilities, only the first 100 are listed. Try selecting Common Words Only, to reduce the number.

37

Beware

Words from the clue may not help if you are completing a cryptic crossword, since they may not appear in the literal definitions.

Crosswords online

The Internet doesn't just help you solve crosswords, it is also a rich source of crosswords. You will soon find your own favorite sites, but to help get you started, try one of the newspapers. For example:

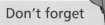

1 Type **www.washingtonpost.com/crosswords** on the address bar and press Enter to open the web page.

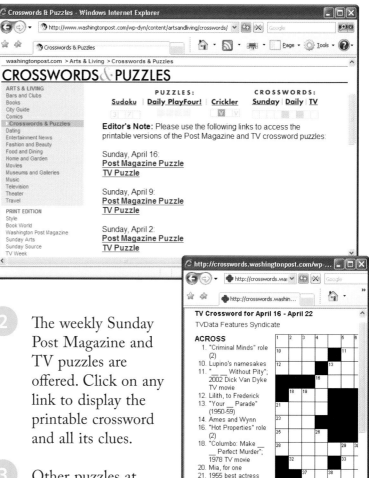

2 The weekly Sunday Post Magazine and TV puzzles are offered. Click on any link to display the printable crossword and all its clues.

3 Other puzzles at this website can be tackled on the PC, while you are online (see page 39).

Interactive crosswords

You can complete some crosswords interactively, but you may need to allow an Add-on to Internet Explorer.

1 Click Daily Crosswords at the Washington Post website.

2 You may be asked to enable an Add-on, in order to try out the puzzle online. Click the link offered.

The interactive crossword is not available on the web browser that you are using since it requires Java. Your web browser does not support Java or Java is not enabled.

? Help

Add-on Disabled
This webpage is requesting an add-on that is disabled. To enable the add-on, click here.

Internet   100%

Beware

Only allow Add-ons for websites that you know and trust. In this case, the Java Plug-in is required.

 Java Plug-in 1.3.1_15 f...

See page 170 for more information on Internet security.

39

3 Select a square, then select the Across or Down clue and type in the letters for your answer.

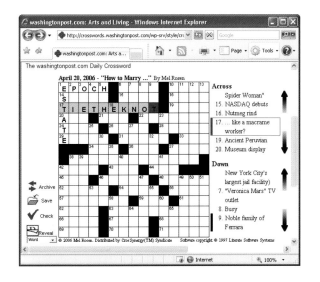

Don't forget

If all else fails, click the Reveal button to show the selected letter or word, or to display the whole solution.

Reveal
Word
Letter
Word
All

4 Click Check to validate your answers, click Save to record progress so far and click Archive to view and solve crosswords from previous days.

✔ Check

🗁 Save

⮂ Archive

Sudoku

If you want a change from crosswords, you might switch to Sudoku. The Internet will provide advice and suggestions for completing the puzzles you find in magazines, and offer puzzles for you to play online or print out to complete later.

 Go to **www.websudoku.com** which claims to have billions of Sudoku puzzles for you to play.

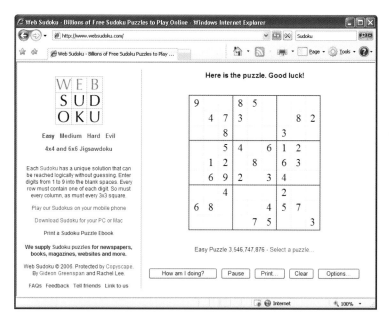

40

 Select Easy, Medium, Hard or Evil to match your skill level or desire for challenge.

 Click an empty cell and type the appropriate digit, based on the contents of other cells. Your entries are in blue italics.

 To check your progress, click **How am I doing?** You'll be warned if you've entered a wrong number.

Solving puzzles

Here are some useful websites that explain some of the techniques involved in solving Sudoku puzzles.

1 At **www.simetric.co.uk/sudoku** you'll find three tutorials that demonstrate solving Sudoku puzzles.

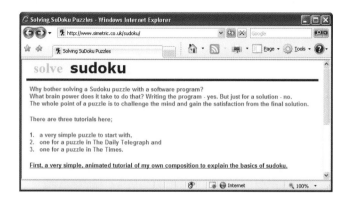

2 There's a comprehensive guide to solving Sudoku, at **www.sudoku.org.uk/PDF/Solving_Sudoku.pdf**.

3 Finally, for the count of valid Sudoku grids, see **www.afjarvis.staff.shef.ac.uk/sudoku/sudoku.pdf**.

Brain aerobics

Brain teasers, quizzes and games are not just for fun or to pass the time, they also provide essential mental exercise.

1 Search for **brain teasers for seniors** to find sites such as **www.clevelandseniors.com/forever/mindex.htm**.

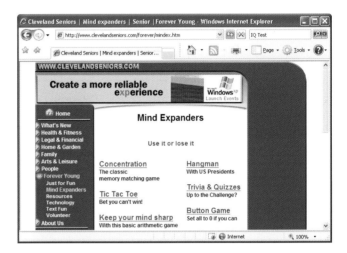

2 Select one of the 15 or so links of Mind Expanders, for example Concentration or Trivia & Quizzes.

3 If you want more cerebral exercise, visit website **www.mensa.org** and click **Mensa Workout**.

Web encyclopedia

To help you answer all the quizzes you find, you'll need good reference material. Make a start with the Web encyclopedia that you can edit and update, as well as reference.

1 Go to **www.wikipedia.org** and choose your preferred language, e.g. English.

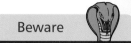

English
The Free Encyclopedia
1 087 000+ articles
Español
La enciclopedia libre
110 000+ artículos

2 Select the Main Page, and scroll down to see the list of sister projects, also user-maintained.

3 Click **Sign in / Create Account** to specify your user name, password and (optionally) your email address. It isn't essential to create an account, but it does let you communicate with other Wikipedia users.

Beware

In principle anybody can contribute to Wikipedia. In practice, older articles tend to be more comprehensive and balanced, while newer articles may contain misinformation or unencyclopedic info, or even vandalism.

Don't forget

Wikipedia is hosted by the Wikimedia Foundation, a non-profit organization that also hosts a range of other projects.

Hot tip

This article illustrates one way of exploring Wikipedia – by trial and error. It was displayed after clicking on the link Random Article several times.

Internet Public Library

The Internet Public Library (IPL), managed and maintained by the University of Michigan School of Information, offers library services to Internet users, helping them to find, evaluate and organize information resources.

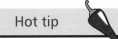

Hot tip

The IPL provides an annotated collection of high quality internet resources, selected by the IPL staff as providing accurate and factual information.

 Visit **www.ipl.org** to see subject collections, ready reference and reading room material, etc.

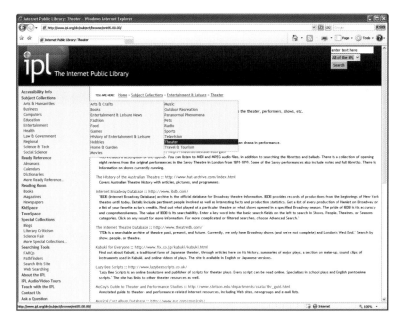

Don't forget

To change resolution, right-click the desktop, select Properties, click the Settings tab, and drag the Screen Resolution slider.

Screen resolution

Less ——————— More

1280 by 1024 pixels

44

2 There's so much information, a high screen resolution may be useful, but this makes the text rather small.

3 Click the Zoom button at the bottom, to switch between 100%, 125%, 150% and back to 100%.

4 Click the down-arrow to choose a preset level, or to choose Custom and set a particular level.

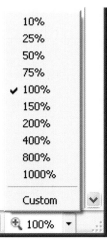

Online classics

You can find the full text for many thousands of books on the Internet, in an electronic (ebook) format that is ideal for searching for particular details. They are books whose copyright has expired, and in the main they are classics. There are online books on Wikipedia and on IPL, but perhaps the best source for free ebooks is Project Gutenberg.

Hot tip

You can participate in Project Gutenberg, for example by volunteering to proof read individual pages of books.

1. Type **www.gutenberg.org** and press Enter to display the home page for the website.

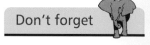

Beware

If you don't live in the US, you should check the copyright laws in your country before downloading an ebook.

2. Click **Online Book Catalog**, and locate books by author or by title.

3. Click **Recent Books** or **Top 100**, to view lists of books in those categories.

Don't forget

You can also browse the database, by author or by title, arranged alphabetically.

4. Advanced Search allows you to search for books with specific words in the text.

Online reference

When it's reference books you want, visit the Bartleby website, where you can access a wide range of well known books.

1 Go to **www.bartleby.com** and click the down-arrow next to the Search box to choose the specific type.

2 You can search the whole site, or a specific section (reference, verse, fiction, or non-fiction), or just in one particular book in a section.

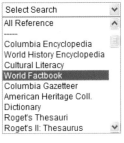

3 To search a subsection of the references, click the Reference link and

then select Encyclopedia, Dictionary, Thesaurus, Quotations, or English Usage. Quotations for example, searches within four collections.

4 Chess and Bridge

Even if you are home alone, you can participate in games of chess or of bridge over the Internet. You can play against the computer or against human opponents. You can watch others play, historical games or live events. You'll also get lots of help on the Internet to improve your game.

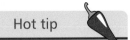

Chess games

Chessgames.com is an online database of historic chess games that help chess players to develop their games.

1. To find a game, go to **www.chessgames.com** to display the home page, with several search options.

2. Type a plain text game description in the search box, for example the player names, and the year, the result or the opening move.

3. Alternatively, fill in the fields on the Advanced Search form:
   - Year
   - Player
   - White or Black
   - Opposing player
   - No. of moves
   - Opening (name)
   - ECO code
   - Result

4. Click the **Find Chess Games** button. The matching games will be listed. Click the game you want to see.

Overall record: Garry Kasparov beat Veselin Topalov 14 to 6, with 16 draws.*
* Based on games present in our database; may not be complete.

Game		Result	Moves	Year	Event/Locale	Opening
1. Kasparov vs Topalov		1-0	44	1999	It (cat.17), Wijk aan Zee (Netherlands)	B06 Robatsch

View game

A chess board will be displayed, along with the list of moves that make up that particular game.

Beware

You'll need the Java add-on enabled (see page 174), and you may have to switch Java Viewers to find the one that works best on your system.

Don't forget

The board shows the current positions for all the chess pieces in play, at any stage in the game.

① Click the arrows to step forward or backward through the game, one move at a time.

② Click one of the double arrows, to move to the start point or to the end point of the game.

③ Click anywhere in the table, to view the state of play at that stage.

Hot tip

The games are stored using PGN (Portable Game Notation), a simple text format which you can download and import to Chess software running on your PC.

Play computer

Studying chess games is educational, but you really need to play games in order to improve your skill level. There are many websites where you can play other people, friends or strangers, but perhaps you could start off playing against a computer program, such as Little Chess Partner.

Hot tip

This is a German site, with English translations, and the usual rules of chess apply, so language isn't a problem.

1 Go to **www.chessica.de/gamezone.html** and click the first Play button, to play against the computer.

Don't forget

You'll need the Java add-on enabled in the browser (see page 174) to play this computer. Once the pieces are displayed, you can play games offline, without an active Internet connection.

50

2 Click the board to start, then drag to move a (white) chess piece turn by turn. The computer won't let you make an illegal move.

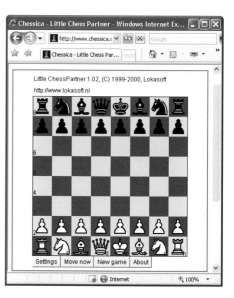

Hot tip

By default, thinking time is 10 seconds and depth of analysis is level 5. Experiment with other values, to make it easier or harder to play.

3 Click **Settings** to change the thinking time or the depth of analysis used by the computer.

If you find the Little Chess Partner too challenging, there's
an easier program that you can play against, to get practise.

① Scroll down and click the link **Try This!** which
appears below the chess board display (see page 50).

② Choose Black or White
for the computer, and
then take your turn by
selecting a piece (which
changes to purple) then
clicking the destination
to make your moves.
Only legal moves will be
allowed.

③ The Game Log records
all the moves made.

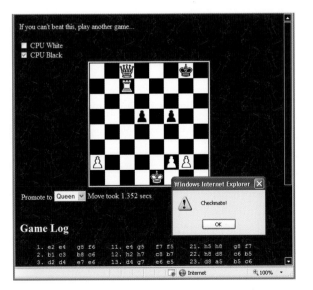

Don't forget

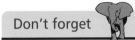

The web author
suggests, somewhat
provocatively, if you
cannot beat this
computer program,
then perhaps you
should try playing a
different type of game.

Hot tip

Select both Black and
White for the CPU,
and it will launch
an automatic game,
showing you the
moves in the Log.
Useful to get ideas
for opening moves,
but it usually ends
in Stalemate, as you
might expect.

51

Chess server

To introduce yourself to the world of chess on the Internet, you could visit the Free Internet Chess Server (FICS).

 Go to **www.freechess.org** to register, login, download interfaces and get help and guidance.

Click the **Downloads** link to look for a graphical interface, the easiest way to connect to FICS.

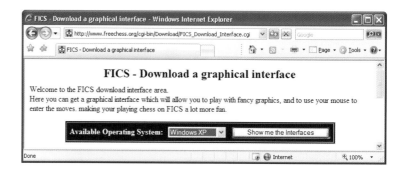

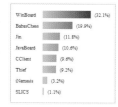

WinBoard	(32.1%)
BabasChess	(19.9%)
Jin	(11.8%)
JavaBoard	(10.6%)
CClient	(9.6%)
Thief	(9.2%)
Nemesis	(3.2%)
SLICS	(1.1%)

Select your operating system (e.g. Windows XP) and click the button **Show me the Interfaces**.

Click the URL for the one you want to try out, e.g. **www.tim-mann.org/xboard.html** for WinBoard.

Graphical interface

You can download a copy of Winboard to your computer, from Tim Mann's chess pages.

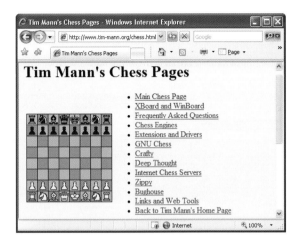

Hot tip

XBoard runs on Unix systems, while WinBoard runs on Windows. Tim Mann is the primary author of both applications.

1 Click the **XBoard and WinBoard** link and scroll down for the download link and other details.

Don't forget

Select to use WinBoard as the viewer for .PGN files (Portable Game Notation – see page 49) and for .FEN files (Forsyth-Edwards Notation).

2 Click the **Download** link and select Save to add winboard-4_2_7a.exe to your downloads folder. Double-click this file to install WinBoard.

3 The WinBoard folder on the Start menu includes an entry for Freechess.com, the FICS server, along with other chess servers and various games that you can view.

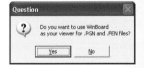

Visit server

You can visit the club as a guest, to help you decide if you'd like to become a full member.

1 Select Start, All Programs, WinBoard, and click the **Chess Server – freechess.org** entry.

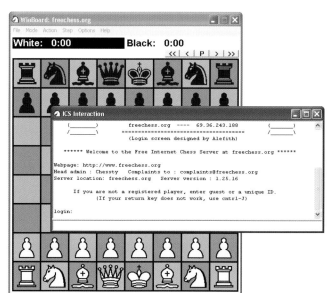

2 Type **guest** and press Enter. FICS will give you a unique ID, in this case GuestNNST.

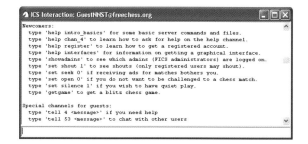

3 Soon you'll start receiving copies of messages from other guests seeking opponents to play. Type **play nn** (where nn is the game number specified) to respond.

Observe games

You may see a message to indicate games are being relayed.

 Type **tell relay listgames** and press Enter.

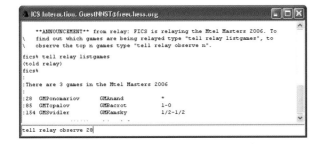

Type **tell relay observe 28** to view that game.

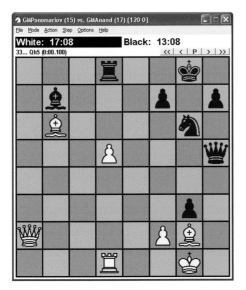

The WinBoard displays the current position for the selected game, then continues to display all the moves as the game proceeds.

Type **help intro_basics** for a list of basic commands, and type **help intro_welcome** for additional details.

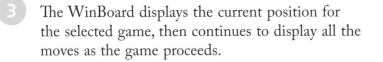

Great Bridge Links

If bridge is your game, it is well supported on the Internet. There's an organized list of bridge-related websites at the nicely named Great Bridge Links.

1 Visit the website **www.greatbridgelinks.com**. The main sets of links are listed at the top of the screen.

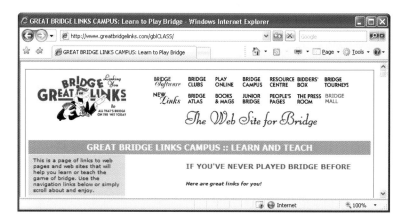

2 Click **Bridge Campus** for links to web pages and websites that will help you learn (or teach) the game of bridge. If you are new to bridge, there's a lesson for complete beginners at Richard Pavlicek's teaching site **www.rpbridge.net/1a00.htm**.

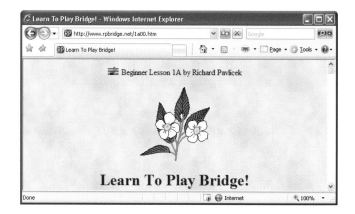

If you already play bridge, you might want to visit one of the more comprehensive sites listed, for example:

1 Visit Karen Walker's Bridge Library at website **www.prairienet.org/bridge** to investigate her collection of class handouts and reference sheets.

2 The American Contract Bridge League has a home page at **www.acbl.org/**, with information and news.

3 For Canadian players, there's Welcome to the World of Bridge at **www.cbf.ca/welcome**, sponsored by the Canadian Bridge Federation.

Online Bridge clubs

When you are ready to play Bridge online, you'll find numerous websites to help you get started and find partners.

1 On Great Bridge Links, click **Play Online** for a list of online Bridge clubs, where individuals can play bridge against others from around the world, of all levels and experience.

2 Click the **Go** button next to an online club, for example **Bridge Base Online**, to display details of the club.

3 Click the website address provided, to visit the club.

CONTACT INFORMATION

Bridge Base Online
New Website:
onlinebridgebase.com

4 Click either **Download** or **Click here to become a member,** to begin the procedure to join the club.

Download software

To join Bridge Base Online (BBO) you need to download and install the associated software on your PC.

1 Select an option to download the file. There are several methods proposed, in case of problems.

2 Click **Run** to download and install the software.

3 Follow the prompts, and accept the default locations and settings.

4 Double click the desktop shortcut, or select the Start menu entry, to log in to **Bridge Base Online**, or to view bridge movies on your computer (see page 62).

Bridge Base
Online

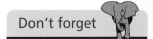

Don't forget

You can choose to Save the file to your hard disk then double-click the downloaded file to run the program later. See page 147.

Beware

You may get a security warning that the publisher could not be verified. If you have any doubts, select Don't Run, then Save the file as noted above and scan for viruses before installing.

59

Hot tip

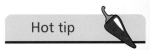

You cannot play bridge at Bridge Base Online directly from the website – you must log in using the downloaded software.

Bridge movies

A Bridge Movie is an interactive presentation, based on a bridge book, article, quiz or match. To view a movie:

 Click **Open Bridge Movie from your computer,** pick an entry from the folder displayed, and press Open.

00ittsf8.lin

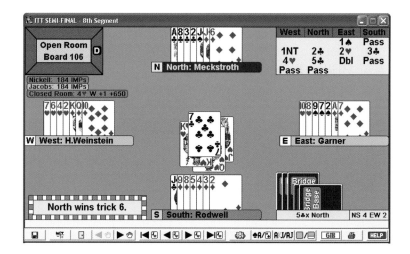

 Click an entry to display the deal and the bidding.

 Click the **Next Page** button to step through the hand. Select Next Board to review more deals.

Log in to BBO

When you log in to Bridge Base Online, you'll need a user name and password, available via the New Member option.

1 Click **Log in to Bridge Base Online**, enter a user name and password, and press the New Member button.

2 Add any details you wish, then click OK.

3 You'll be told if your user name is already in use, so you can try a different one. When you have a unique user name, you are allowed into the lobby, from where you can play and improve your bridge.

Hot tip

If you click the Log in as invisible box, your name will not appear in the lobby list, but if you go to a table or enter a chat room, you will become visible.

Don't forget

Values for your real name, your email address, and your country are required (many members leave them as the default Private). Your skill level and Other information are optional and can be added later.

Beware

The details you provide will be visible to all members, so provide limited details until you are sure you want to remain a member.

Kibitz a table

You can join a table as an observer and watch the game. This is referred to as kibitzing.

Play Bridge!
Click to play or watch!

1 Click the **Play Bridge** button, and then enter the main bridge club (as recommended for new users).

Play Bridge!
1576 Tables 7716 Players

56º Suramericano de Bridge
9 al 16 de septiembre de 2006
www.bridgecolombia.com Cartagena, Colombia

Places to play	Click to enter the Main Bridge Club (recommended for new members)	
Main Bridge Club	731	3120
Private Bridge Clubs	10	42
Public Bridge Clubs	29	137
Tournaments	657	2931
Team Matches	124	1391
Play bridge for money!	25	95

2 The first time you kibitz, find a table that already has several kibitzers, and that doesn't require permission.

Bridge Base Online - Main Bridge Club

Main Bridge Club   **736 Tables 728 Displayed**

Host	North	South	East	West	Kibitzers	Scoring	Description
ausoleil	ausoleil	asherp12	banakayyal	janjoun	0	IMP Pairs	avancés sef francophon
auve	alfj	auve	henrikt	EvaLund	3	IMP Pairs	
avenay	avenay	laideron	barbarag	amulz	0	IMP Pairs	
Click to kibitz at awm1's table ki			Karayel 1	kemin	0	IMP Pairs	
awm1	zadic	daniel84	mustapha	awm1	0	IMP Pairs	
babadi	sidonie48	babadi	Huseyin54	stanes33	0	IMP Pairs	

3 You view the game as a bridge movie (see page 60). Press Back to leave the table.

BACK

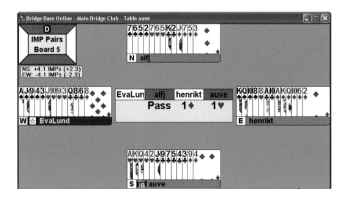

5 Internet Entertainment

Use the Internet as your TV and Radio guide, to see what's on the regular channels or to tune into web broadcasts. Check what movies are being released, and what shows are on stage around the world. Or just relax to the sound of classical music.

What's on TV?

Every country has its national and regional television stations, along with numerous local stations. The Internet can help you keep track of them, and even look in on them, since many offer websites and broadcast over the Internet.

Hot tip

The TV data streams, available live or on demand from the websites, require bandwidth from 28.8 Kbps (modem rate) up to 1500 Kbps (broadband rates).

64

1 Start with a visit to a TV Station directory such as **wwitv.com** which lists live and on-demand TV broadcasts from around the world.

Don't forget

When you want to view web stations, you can look anywhere in the world, not just your local area or region.

2 Scroll down and select a location, the UK for example, to list all the TV stations available.

TURKEY
U. KINGDOM
UKRAINE

Hot tip

The listing includes the website and a description of the type of content for each of the TV stations in the specified location.

	Website (source)	Stream	Stream	Live?	Information
SWEDEN 9					
SWITZERLAND 13	3BTV	200K	340K	Y	WebTV only.
SYRIA 1					
TAIWAN 14	BBC 2			Y	Recorded news.
THAILAND 19					
TUNESIA 3	BBC 4			n	Recorded items available on
TURKEY 35					website.
U. KINGDOM 55					Roundup of the
UKRAINE 4	BBC Sport			n	latest sports
UN. ARAB EM. 3					news.
URUGUAY 5					
USA (A-F) 68	BBC Weather	80K		n	Weather forecast for the UK.
USA (G-L) 56					
USA (M-T) 75					Weekly news and
USA (U-Z) 53	BBC_Breakfast			n	current affairs
UZBEKISTAN 2	with Frost				programme.
VATICAN CITY 2					
VENEZUELA 8					

Broadband TV

If you want to view online, you can limit the list to only those stations offering a direct data stream.

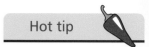
Hot tip

 Click **Broadband TV** and reselect the country or location you want to list.

| all tv channels | broadband tv | movie&video | speedtest |

Broadband TV selects stations that broadcast at 200 Kbps or higher, unsuitable for dial-up modem connections, which are at best limited to about 45 Kbps.

Choose a stream to view – Green if you use the Windows Media Player, Blue for the RealPlayer, and Grey for the WinAmp player.

Don't forget

To install one of the players, click Required Software. The site will detect which players are already installed, and give you the options to download any of the others.

View the streamed program in the associated software, in this case **Windows Media Player**.

Regular TV

Even if you want to watch regular TV (satellite, cable or antenna), the Internet proves useful for searching schedules.

Hot tip

TV Zap offers a range of websites providing schedules and guides for the country or region you select, outlining the type of content so you can decide which will suit you best.

66

① TV Zap has links to worldwide television schedules and guides, at the **www.tvzap.com** website.

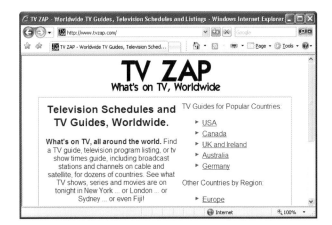

Don't forget

The television schedule may be presented as part of a larger website devoted to the particular country or region. Look out for links such as TV Guides or Television Schedules.

② Select the country or region you are interested in, e.g. Canada, to list the relevant guides and schedules.

③ Choose one of the TV Schedule websites, specify the time period, category and keywords, then follow the prompts to see the schedule for your location.

What's on radio?

You can find out what's on terrestrial radio stations, and listen to radio stations that broadcast over the Internet.

1   Type the web address **radiostationworld.com** in the browser address bar.

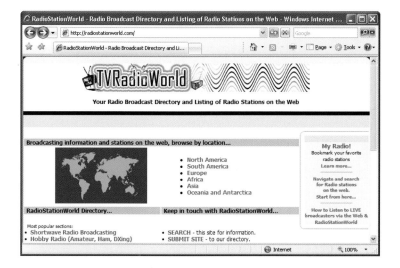

2   Click the link **Navigate** and search for radio stations, select the location from the table and then click Go.

Navigate and search
for Radio stations
on the web.
Start from here...

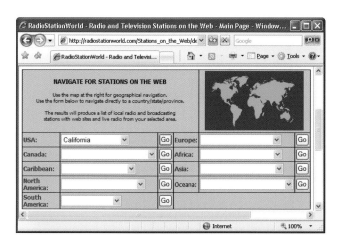

Hot tip

The original address for this website was TVRadioWorld. com and this will still display the site. However, the emphasis has now switched to radio broadcasts.

Don't forget

As with TV over the Internet (see page 65) you'll need a player to listen to the broadcast programs.

Internet radio

The towns and regions in the selected state or country are listed, with links to the lists of their local radio stations (with the number of stations shown after the link, e.g. [#81]).

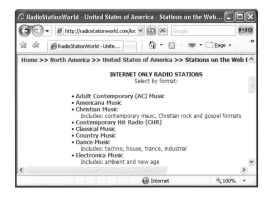

68

1   Click the Webcasters link to list only those stations that broadcast on the Internet.

2   If you select Internet Only (see page 69) for the USA, it will list the web stations by content category.

Internet Radio, Canada
✛ ◀ BUZZRadio
✛ ◀ CBC Radio 3
✛ ◀ Dox Radio
✛ ◀ Iceberg Radio
✛ ◀ Radio Rumberos
✛ ◀ Swing2jazz

Select a category, for example Classical Music, to list the stations available for that format.

1 Click the speaker symbol for a particular station to start listening to that broadcast.

2 If a choice of software is offered, select your preferred media player.

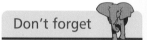
Hot tip

There are twenty or so different categories of radio stations listed, based on the type of content and presentation format.

Don't forget

Click the [+] button to add the station to your My Radio list, a sort of favorites list maintained for you by Radio Station World.

Hot tip

Normally, the stations will support one or more of the same media players used for TV broadcasts (see page 65).

Visit the BBC

You can visit particular broadcasters, such as CNN, NBC or the BBC, to see what features they have to offer.

1   Visit the BBC website at **www.bbc.co.uk** and select the UK version or the International version as appropriate to you.

2   Click the Radio tab to see the stations and programs available, and to listen in to broadcasts.

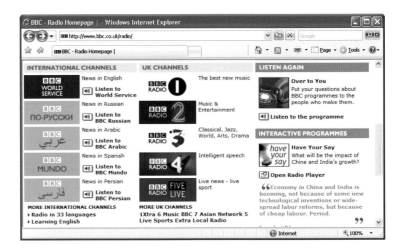

3   Click the speaker icon to listen to a station, or click a channel logo to visit the home page for that station.

Hollywood movies

Maybe movies are your preference. As you'd expect, the Internet has lots to say about them. For many people, the home of movies is in Hollywood, California.

1 You'll find a comprehensive list of Hollywood movies at the **www.hollywood.com** website.

2 Click the **Movie Calendar** link to see what movies have been released or are planned for future months.

3 If your interest is in Indian and Asian movies, visit the alternative movie website at **www.bollywoodworld.com**.

Don't forget

As usual, you can right-click the link and select Open Link in New Tab, rather than a separate window.

71

Hot tip

Click the month to list movies for that period, and click the movie title for details and reviews.

New York theater

If all the world's a stage for you, visit the theater websites to see what shows are on.

72

1. For New York City theater information, including show listings, look at **www.theatre.com**.

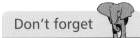
2. Click the **see venue listings** link to list Broadway and off-Broadway venues in Manhattan's Theatre District (between 34th and 59th Streets).

3. Click the underlined theater name to find out more about that venue, including details such as exact location, travel directions and the seating plan. Click the show title to find out more about the show itself.

London theater guide

If you are planning to be in London, you can check what's on in the West End, at the Official London Theatre site.

1 The **www.officiallondontheatre.co.uk** website has theater news, show lists, ticket purchase awards etc.

2 Click **Theatreland Map** and select the **GIF** link to view the map as an image in the browser.

3 Select the **PDF** link to download a higher resolution map and view or print it with Adobe Reader in IE7.

Hot tip

If the map is displayed reduced size, to fit in the browser window, click with the Expand Image cursor to see it full size.

Don't forget

If Internet Explorer offers to download the file, you do not have the Adobe Reader installed. See page 74 to add this to your system.

Install Adobe Reader

Adobe Reader may be installed (at no cost) from Adobe's website.

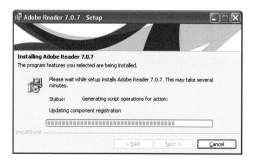

1. Visit **www.adobe.com** and click the button labeled Get Adobe reader.

2. Click the **Download** button for the latest version of Adobe Reader, and follow the prompts.

3. Adobe Reader is installed, and Internet Explorer is reconfigured to use Adobe Reader for PDF files.

4. When you click on a link to an online PDF document, it will now open in Internet Explorer.

Classical music archives

If you'd simply like to relax to the sound of classical music, the Internet will not disappoint you.

1   Visit **www.classicalarchives.com** to find a collection of music that you can listen to – without charge.

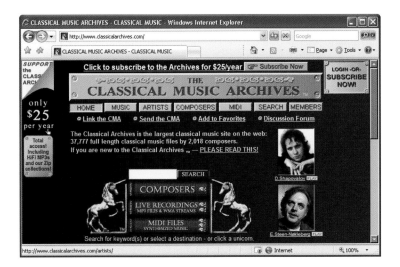

2   Click the **Play** button for one of the sample pieces to make sure they will play on your system.

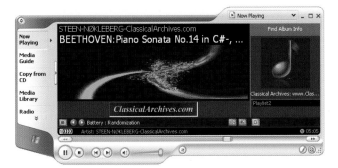

3   Click **Please Read This,** then scroll down to the **Register Here** link.

Hot tip

Registered Free Members can play up to five pieces per day. For an annual fee of $25, subscribers are allowed up to 100 plays a day.

Hot tip

The online music is in Windows Media Player format, but subscribers can also save files in MP3 format.

Don't forget

There are several links for paid subscribers, but free registration is buried in the details of the Introduction.

...cont'd

Hot tip

Membership is free. No payment is needed, and no credit card details are asked for or required.

Beware

Replying to the email will not activate your membership. You must click on the link provided, to complete your registration.

Don't forget

There are nearly forty thousand pieces from over two thousand composers stored in the classical music archives.

To register at the Classical Music Archive, you provide your name, email address, password, location and phone number.

 When you've completed the form, click the **Free Member Registration** button to submit your details.

An email is sent to the address you specify. Click the web link provided, to activate membership.

Click to **Return to the Archives' Home Page**, and select from the list of great composers, or from the complete alphabetic list of composers provided.

6 Arts and Crafts

Whether you want to view pictures and drawings by contemporary artists or old masters, or get help and advice for creating your own works of art, the Internet has information and a host of tutorials to help you improve your skills.

Web Gallery of Art

The Web Gallery of Art is a virtual museum and searchable database of European painting and sculpture:

 Go to the website **www.wga.hu** and click the **Enter Here** button.

ENTER HERE

 Type the artist and title (e.g. Vermeer, Girl with a Pearl Earring) and the date or format if known, then press **Search** to find matching pictures.

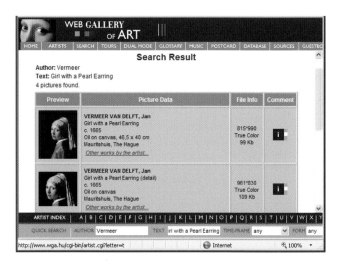

Visit the Sistine Chapel

To see the features of the Gallery in action, it is useful to take one of the predefined guided tours.

Tour #5: Visit to the Sistine Chapel in Vatican

Description: *This tour guides you through the Sistine Chapel in the Vatican, presenting the ceiling frescoes painted by Michelangelo between 1508 and 1512, the Last Judgment, the largest single fresco created in the 16th century, also by Michelangelo between 1535 and 1541, and the frescoes on the side walls painted by different, mainly Florentine artists in the 15th century.*

Sources: CAMESASCA, Ettore, *L'Opera completa di Michelangelo pittore*, Rizzoli Editore, Milano, 1966; VECCHI, Pierluigi de, COLALUCCI, Gianluigi, *Michelangelo -The Vatican Frescoes*, Abbeville Press Publishers, New York, London, 1996; BARTZ, Gabriele, KÖNIG, Eberhard, *Michelangelo*, Könemann, Cologne, 1998; SCHOTT, Rolf, *Michelangelo*, Thames and Hudson Limited, London, 1964; HEUSINGER, Lutz, *Michelangelo*, Scala/Riverside, New York, 1989

 Click the title of the tour you wish to take, for example **Visit to the Sistine Chapel** in the Vatican.

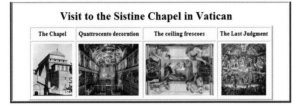

Select a section of the tour to see detailed images and instructive comments.

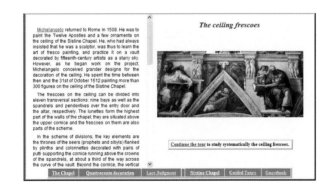

Note that some sections may be further subdivided.

Hot tip

Click the Tours button to show brief details of the guided tours available.

Don't forget

There are 15 different tours defined on the website, including:
#1 Italian painters
#2 European sculptors
#3 Art of Giotto
#4 Frescoes at Arezzo
#5 Sistine Chapel
#6 Brancacci Chapel

Hot tip

This tour shows how you click parts of the image to zoom in and see details and explanations. Other tours demonstrate more facilities such as dual mode (side by side) presentations.

Water color painting

If you are interested in learning to paint in water color, or want to develop your skill, there are websites to help you.

1 At **www.watercolorpainting.com** there are tutorials, step by step guides and lots of art related links.

Don't forget

Hold down Shift and Ctrl as you click the Tutorials link, to open it in a new IE tab and switch to that tab.

2 Click the **Tutorials** tab for an introduction to water color painting and for basic and advanced tutorials.

3 Click **Paintings** for step by step painting guides, explaining the materials and the techniques used.

Learn to draw

Perhaps you've always wanted to draw, but never had the time. Now may be just the time to begin.

1 Search for the phrase **learn to draw** for a list of websites related to this topic.

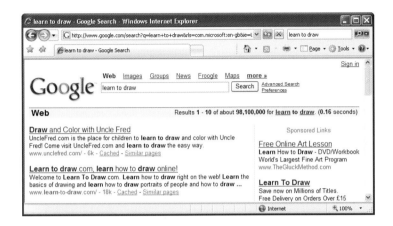

2 Select **www.learn-to-draw.com**, to get sets of easy to follow instructions for a variety of drawing tasks.

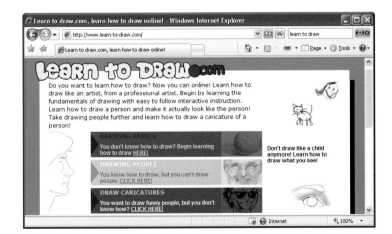

3 Pick the tutorial that suits your existing skill level.

Don't forget

There are certain to be many websites offered. Some are purely for profit, some are there just to share an interest, while others turn out to be a mixture of both.

Beware

The Drawing Basics instructions are free, but the later topics in Drawing People and Draw Caricatures are available only to subscribers (who pay a one-time $15 charge).

DRAWING PEOPLE
Introduction
problems
materials
the profile
drawing eyes
finish the profile
symmetry
straight on face
measuring
the eyes
the nose
the mouth
the smile
hair
3 quarters

Pen and ink drawing

There's a "step-by-step" tutorial available on the Virtual Portmeirion website that tells you how to produce pen and ink drawings based on photographs.

1   Visit **www.virtualportmeirion.com/howto/** to see the list of steps involved in creating the drawing.

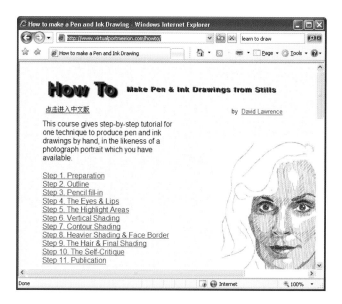

2   You will need some suitable drawing tools:
- An extra fine black rolling ball pen
- A black felt tip pen
- A black broad tip magic marker
- A regular HB grade pencil
- A blue leaded pencil (blue doesn't photocopy)

3   Each step contains detailed advice, with lots of useful tips and illustrative sketches. For example, in step 4 you learn how to draw eyes with reflective areas and positioned so that the subject is looking in the right direction.

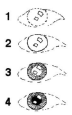

Origami

What will you do with all that paper from your painting and drawing practise? Origami, the art of paper folding, sounds the natural thing to try next.

 1 As usual, search for related sites by typing a keyword such as **origami** in the Search box.

2 Go to **origami.iap-peacetree.org/basic_folds.php** to see the basic folds.

3 The Origami folds include:
Valley
Mountain
Petal
Rabbit Ear
Squash
Reverse (in)
Reverse (out)
Crimp
Sink

Celtic knots

Celtic knots are motifs created by loops or continuous threads. They can be found on ancient stonework and in illuminated manuscripts, and in the form of jewellery and tattoos. You can also design and draw them on paper.

Beware

Associations such as Love, Loyalty or Friendship assigned to Celtic knot designs are inventions. The spiritual meanings of ancient symbols have been lost, while more recent symbols are merely decorative.

1 Go to **www.aon-celtic.com,** click the **Knotwork** link, then click the **Basic Celtic Knotwork** tutorial.

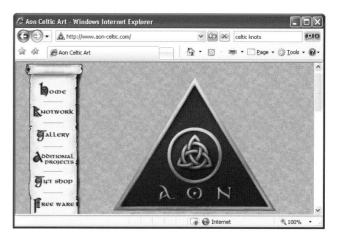

Don't forget

This website adds a new tutorial each month, covering different types of Celtic knots, to encourage repeat visits.

2 Follow the steps in the tutorial to mark up a piece of graph paper, joining the sections and the corners then deleting lines where threads overlap.

You can draw Celtic knots in your browser, with the help of applications provided over the Internet.

1 Click the box to create and extend Celtic knots at **www.entrelacs.net/SquareKnot/SquareKnot.html**.

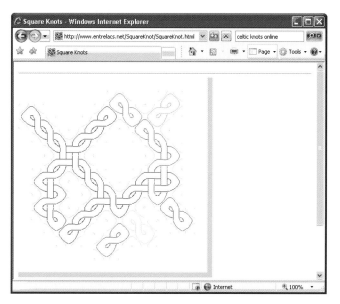

Beware

This address is case sensitive. The capital letters in SquareKnot are required.

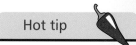
Hot tip

Click cross-overs or adjacent segments to change the ways they are connected. This method applies to both applications.

85

2 For **www.bit-101.com/celticknots** click Draw to generate the Celtic knot as defined by the settings.

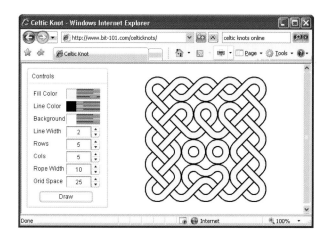

Don't forget

Drag the color sliders to change settings for Fill, Line and Background colors.

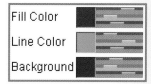

You can also set line width, number of rows and columns, rope width and grid space.

Cross stitch

If your preference is for textiles and threads, you can find tutorials and patterns galore. These are often free of charge, even on websites that are online shops.

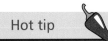

Hot tip

This website offers organic and fair trade alternatives for babies, adults and pets, but it does not sell cross stitch patterns and materials, so these are genuinely free.

1 Visit the site **www. crossstitch.com** to display the free cross stitch patterns that are offered.

2 Click on the image to display links for the pattern sheets.

Don't forget

The threads required are specified using DMC stranded cotton shade numbers.

86

Free cross stitch pattern
Hummingbird in Flight

Eastern Tiger Swallowtail Butterfly
Free Cross Stitch Pattern
If you are new to cross-stitch, you can learn from the
Counted Cross Stitch Tutorial

Texas bluebonnet cross stitch pattern

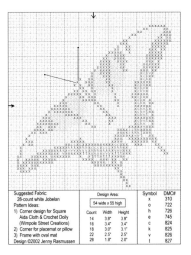

Suggested Fabric: 28-count white Jobelan	Design Area:		Symbol	DMC#
Pattern Ideas:	54 wide x 55 high		x	310
1) Corner design for Square			o	722
Aida Cloth & Crochet Doily	Count	Width	Height	h	726
(Wimpole Street Creations)	14	3.9"	3.9"	e	745
2) Corner for placemat or pillow	16	3.4"	3.4"	c	824
3) Frame with oval mat	18	3.0"	3.1"	k	825
	22	2.5"	2.5"	v	826
Design ©2002 Jenny Rasmussen	28	1.9"	2.0"	t	827

3 The patterns specify the positions and suggest the most suitable colors for the stitches.

Eastern Tiger Swallowtail
Butterfly

When planning a butterfly garden, remember to use larval food plants.
In Central Texas, an important larval food for the Eastern Tiger Swallowtail
is the Mexican plum, which also provides nectar for butterflies and food for birds.

Bird Cross Stitch Designs by Jenny Rasmussen. Visit Jenny on the web at www.BirdCrossStitch.com

If you are new to cross stitch, a tutorial will help. Many cross stitch websites reference the very comprehensive tutorial written by Kathleen Dyer. To view a copy:

1 Go to **users.rcn.com/kdyer.dnai** and click the **Counted Cross Stitch Tutorial** link.

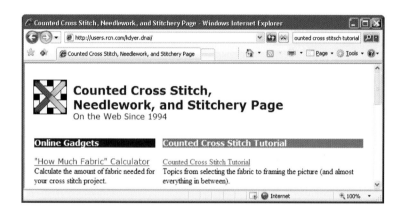

2 The tutorial at **www.celticxstitch.ie/learnhow.html** offers a more graphical approach. They advise using a kit, but do tell you how to select your own materials.

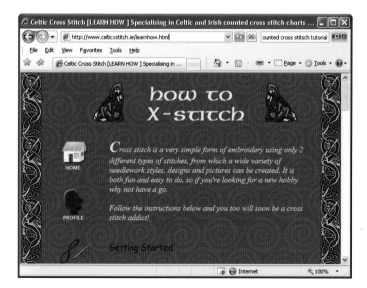

Don't forget

This tutorial covers all aspects of cross stitch, including:
  Selecting the Fabric
  Selecting the Thread
  Selecting the Needle
  Number of Strands
  Making the X
  Fractional Stitches
  Cleaning and Storing
  Mounting / Framing

Hot tip

The Celtic X-stitch tutorial has animated illustrations of the single, block and back stitches used for cross stitching.

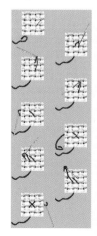

Knitting

If you enjoy knitting and like to make items for charitable causes, you'll find inspiration at websites such as Knitting Patterns Central at **www.knittingpatternscentral.com**.

1 Select the pattern you want to review, for example the **Diamond Lace Bookmark**.

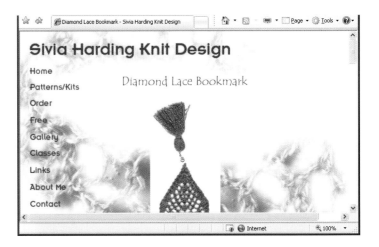

2 This gives details of the materials, full instructions for knitting and finishing, and permission to use the pattern for personal or charity purposes only.

Guilds

Guilds are useful sources of information and let you contact like-minded people, over the Internet or in local meetings.

1 Visit the Knitting Guild Association (TKGA) at **www.tkga.com** and click on **Guilds/Clubs**.

Don't forget

You'll find similar national associations for other countries and for most crafts and hobbies.

89

2 Select **Find a Local Guild/Club** and type your city or state (e.g. **New York**) to obtain a list for your area.

Hot tip

If there is no local guild or club in your area, the TKGA will advise and assist you in setting up your own local guild.

3 The guilds and clubs affiliated with TKGA in your area are listed, with contact names, telephone numbers and email address (where available).

Other crafts

If we haven't covered your favorite craft, search on Google, or explore a website such as **www.about.com** that provides preselected links for particular subjects.

Don't forget

About.com is now owned by the New York Times Company, so you'll find sponsored links and offers of supplies and equipment, but there will also be plenty of free information.

Hot tip

The About.com guide for your selected topic will offer tutorials or projects, regular articles and perhaps a newsletter, plus links to related websites.

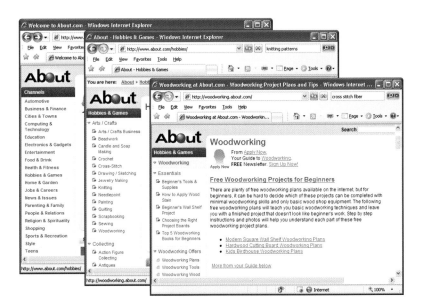

1. Click a category such as **Hobbies & Games**, and then a topic such as **Woodworking**, within the **Arts/Crafts** subcategory.

2. Alternatively, the website **www.allfiberarts.com** covers textile handicrafts, including crochet, dyeing, felting, knitting, sewing, spinning and weaving.

Don't forget

Other topics in the Link Library include:
  Basketry
  Beadwork
  Bobbin Lace
  Classes
  E-Cards
  Kits
  Looms
  Papermaking
  Rug Hooking

7 Travel Plans

The Internet provides you with the tools available to travel agents, so you can search for suitable deals, compare prices offered by different services, and create your own custom vacation. The Internet tells you what's going on at your chosen destination, and gives you maps to help you find your way there.

World wide travel

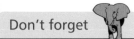

Don't forget

People over 50 make up the majority of travellers worldwide. They have the time and the freedom to travel, and with the help of the Internet, can find options to match their interests and their budgets.

There's a whole wide world of travel options available to you when you start planning a trip. You could be seeking a low cost holiday or have a luxury vacation in mind. You might have plenty of time for research or it could be a last-minute trip. Safety and comfort could be your key consideration or you might be seeking adventure.

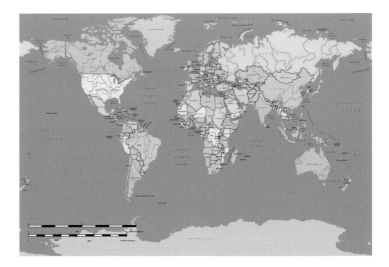

92

Hot tip

Which are the best websites for travel? Each will have its own particular strengths, so it all depends on what aspects you consider important, how much of the work you are ready and able to do for yourself, and what time you have available for planning. We start by looking at the multifunction online travel agent sites (see page 93).

Whatever your requirements, the World Wide Web can help. There are many websites on the Internet devoted to one or more of the various aspects of travel, including:

- Transportation – air, sea, rail, road and river

- Accommodation – hotel, motel, b&b, self catering apartment, recreational vehicle, tent, camp site

- Destinations – domestic, overseas, remote location, single center, multicenter, tour, cruise

- Activities – sun and sand, sight seeing, city break, educational, cultural, sport, adventure, volunteer

- Information – maps, directions, guides, reviews, travel books, Internet access

- Facilities – itineraries, luggage, disabled suitability, currency, passports, adapters

Online travel agents

The most natural choice, when you first start planning vacations on the Internet, is to use the online equivalent of the high street travel agent. There are a number of such websites, but **Expedia** is a popular choice.

1. Go to **www.expedia.com** (or the version for your location) to research, plan and purchase your trip.

2. Select Sign In and, on your initial visit, click Create an Account. Fill in your name, user name, password and your email address.

Beware

You can only purchase tickets and holidays from the version of the website meant for your home location i.e. www.expedia.

com	USA
co.uk	UK
ca	Canada
de	Germany
fr	France
it	Italy
nl	Netherlands
au	Australia

93

Hot tip

If you have signed up for a Microsoft Passport, for example by acquiring a Hotmail account, you can use your Passport.

Hot tip

The next time you visit, sign in using your new user name and password.

Book flights

Most travel plans start with the flights, since these are often the limiting factor, due to their cost or the limited availability of seats on popular or holiday dates.

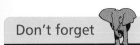

Don't forget

Print off any vouchers for flights or other bookings, to give yourself a record of the reservation number.

Hot tip

Keep a list of airports that you might use, for example:

Antigua	ANY
London	LHR
New York	JFK
Sydney	SYD
Vancouver	YVR

Then put the airport rather than the city.

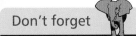

Don't forget

To refine the search, specify the airline, select the class of ticket, and choose nonstop or refundable flights only.

1 At **www.expedia.com**, select Flight, then Leaving From city or airport and Going to city or airport.

2 Set the departure and return dates and times, and select the numbers of adults, seniors (65+) and children.

3 Click **Search for Flights**.

If there's more than one airport for the city, Expedia prompts you with a list, and searches for suitable flights.

Expedia.com is searching for flights on selected travel dates: Wed 10/4/2006 — Wed 10/18/2006

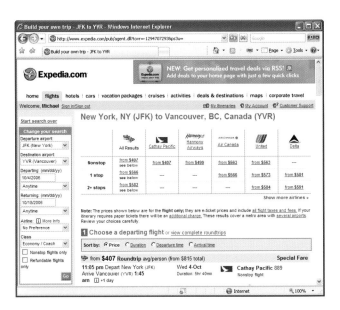

You select your departing flight from the first list, and then select your returning flight from the next list. If you'd prefer to select the two flights at once:

Choose a departing flight or view complete roundtrips

 Click the link **view complete roundtrips,** to show all the combinations of departing and returning flights.

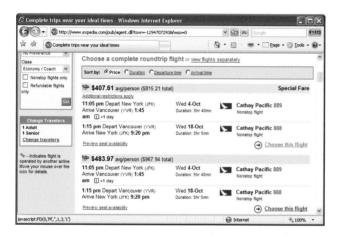

Hot tip

The tickets are not purchased, and the fares are not guaranteed, until you have supplied your credit card details and confirmed the order.

Beware

Take note of messages such as "Additional restrictions apply" (e.g. ticket cannot be amended) or "+1 day" (an overnight flight).

Check the details then click **Choose this flight** for the roundtrip that you wish to book.

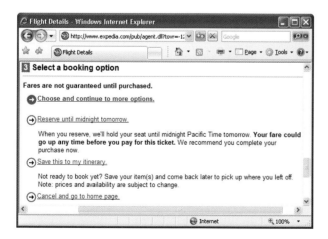

Hot tip

The details will be confirmed, you will be offered the chance to add a hotel or a rental car. Then you can choose to purchase, reserve, save or cancel the booking.

95

Book your hotel

You can choose to book a hotel while you are purchasing your flight tickets, or you can make it a separate transaction.

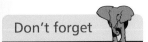
1 At **www.expedia.com**, select Hotel, then the Destination city.

2 Set the check-in and the check-out dates and times, and select the number of rooms and the number of adults and children.

3 Optionally, specify a specific hotel name or class (1 to 5 star).

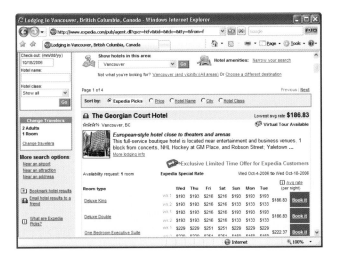

4 Click **Search for hotels** to list the hotels in the vicinity of the city, with room types and rates.

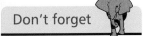
5 Click **Hotel map view** to select your hotel by location.

Hotel list view   Hotel map view

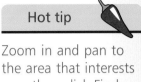

<cite></cite>

Hot tip

Zoom in and pan to the area that interests you, then click Find Lodgings In New View.

Beware

Check the restrictions carefully. You may be required to make full payment, and you may not be able to amend or cancel the booking.

6 Select the hotel that best suits your needs, then click **Book it** to complete the order or save the booking in your itinerary.

Other Hotels

Expedia only searches hotels where it has agreements. For example, it doesn't include hotels from the Intercontinental chain (Holiday Inn etc). For such hotels, you need to book direct with the chain or the specific hotel.

Hot tip

If you book with any Intercontinental hotel, consider joining their Priority Club Rewards scheme. Other hotels have similar schemes (see page 100).

Book a rental car

You can book a rental car along with your flight tickets, or in a separate transaction.

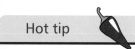

Hot tip

Choose from the list of vehicles in Car type, and Expedia will show cars that size or larger.

1. At **www.expedia.com**, select Car, then the Pick-up location and Car type.

2. Choose the pick-up and the drop-off dates and times, and set additional options such as one-way rentals if appropriate.

3. Click **Search for cars**.

Preferred Vendor View shows cars from companies with whom Expedia has special agreements. The other views show cars from all the available suppliers.

Don't forget

You can also book directly with the car rental company. This may give you better pick-up and drop-off options.

Mid Size Car

Midsize Car shown

Vendor	Doors	Mileage	Location	Weekly rate	Total price*	
Budget	2/4	Unlimited		$169.21	$247.48	Select
Alamo	2/4	Unlimited		$223.86	$321.06	Select
Hertz	2/4	Unlimited		$255.63	$367.05	Select
Thrifty	2/4	Unlimited		$432.93	$605.90	Select
Dollar	2/4	Unlimited	?	$449.84	$623.67	Select
National	2/4	Unlimited		$485.54	$668.30	Select

4. Click **Select** to see the full details for a particular car. Charges are shown in local currency, e.g. $Canadian.

5. Continue the booking to confirm the driver details and book the car, or save the details in your itinerary.

Other online travel agents

Like **Expedia**, the **Travelocity** website helps you book flights, hotels, cars, package vacations and cruises. It produces similar results, but not necessarily identical pricing.

Hot tip

If you have the time, run the same travel query on several of the travel agent websites and explore the differences.

Orbitz, a subsidiary of five American airlines, can book hotels, cars, packages and cruises, as well as flights.

Hot tip

Orbitz is owned by American, Continental, Delta, Northwest and United airlines. This doesn't seem to limit its selections, and it does offer a low fare promise.

LOW FARE PROMISE! Orbitz Low Fare Promise
Find the lowest total airfare online, or get $50 toward your next purchase - GO!

If you are based in Europe, you might consider **Opodo**, set up by nine European airlines, and providing a full range of travel planning services.

Hot tip

Opodo is now owned by the travel company Amadeus and the airlines Aer Lingus, Air France, Alitalia, Austrian Airlines, British Airways, Finnair, Iberia, KLM and Lufthansa.

Loyalty cards

Airlines operate programs to encourage travelers to stay loyal to the particular airline or alliance of airlines. For example, American Airlines operates its own AAdvantage program, and participates in the OneWorld program with British Airways, Cathay Pacific, Qantas and other airlines.

Beware

Keep track of the members of an alliance, since they will change. Aer Lingus is set to withdraw from the OneWorld alliance in 2007, while Japan Airlines, Malév and Royal Jordanian will be joining.

Don't forget

Some booking options from Expedia and other such sites may exclude loyalty card air miles and points, so you should take this into account when selecting between alternatives.

Hotels also offer loyalty programs, which earn miles (in collaboration with airline programs) or points that can be exchanged for accommodation or other goods and services.

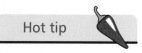

Hot tip

All loyalty programs include elite levels such as silver or gold, awarded when you attain a certain number of air miles or points during the membership year.

Car rental companies also offer loyalty programs, which can be linked to various hotel and airline programs.

Last-minute bookings

Last-minute booking is perhaps the complete antithesis of loyalty programs – you have to take whatever you can get.

1 Visit website **www.priceline.com,** to show all the combinations of departing and returning flights.

2 Enter the details then click **Next** to list the flights available from up to ten airlines.

3 Choose departing and return flights, then enter the passenger details. You'll also be offered the option to rent a car, plus a list of local attractions and services.

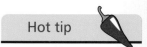

Hot tip

If you can fly any time of day, agree to fly on any major airline, stay in any name-brand hotel or rent from any of the top five US car rental agencies, you might be able to save a lot of money.

Hot tip

There's a similar service to Priceline. com available from www.hotwire.com.

Beware

Prices may rise, even if you are in the middle of confirming the offer. However, you won't be obliged to complete the transaction.

Important

Due to constantly changing availability, the price for this itinerary has increased.

Name your own price

With **Priceline.com** and **Hotwire.com**, you could make a bid for flight by specifying your own price, and seeing if any airline is willing to accept it. Since you provide the price, not the supplier, this is know as a **reverse auction**.

Don't forget
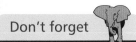

Your flight could start any time between 6am and 10pm on your travel date, so you do need to be very flexible.

Not Flexible?
Choose exact flight times and prices

1 Request flights at **www. priceline.com**, entering the details and clicking **Next**, as described on page 101.

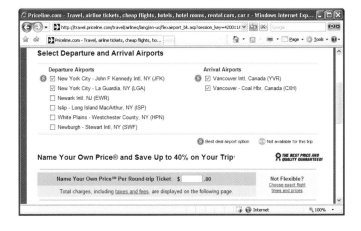

Hot tip

Your price is per round ticket, before taxes and fees. These will be added to the amount that you specify. In the example booking, the extra costs would be $90.50 per person.

2 Choose **Name Your Own Price**, then select the departure and arrival airports you are willing to use.

3 Provide the price that you are willing to pay for the journey that you have specified, and enter the passenger names.

Beware

If the price is too low, your bid is rejected. If any airline is willing to accept your price, your bid will be accepted and your credit card will be charged. You won't know the details until you're fully committed.

4 When you are completely sure that the deal as defined would be acceptable to you, provide your credit card details and complete the bid.

Travel guide

To help you choose your destination and stop off points, you need a travel guide that will tell everything you need to know, laid out in a good and consistent format.

1 Go to **www.mytravelguide.com**, and type your destination e.g. **Vancouver, BC** in the Search box.

2 The guide gives details such as hotels, attractions, restaurants and nearby towns for each location.

3 You will also find a detailed city map.

Hot tip

MyTravelGuide lists related destinations, so you can select the most appropriate one.

Don't forget

MyTravelGuide is owned by Priceline, but it is completely free to use. If you register, you can create quick links and save your itineraries.

Travel directions

If you are planning a multi-stop driving vacation, you'll want travel directions as well as a map. Use a website that allows you to specify intermediate points on your journey.

Beware

Google Maps do not provide for stops. MapQuest will allow up to 10 stops, but this feature is currently in beta testing mode.

1 Click the Sign Me Up button to register for **www.randmcnally.com** and click **Road Explorers.**

2 Click **Sign In** and then click the **Sign Me Up** button to register for basic membership with Rand McNally.

Sign Me Up

3 Provide your first and last name, email address, password, zip or post code, and date of birth.

Don't forget

Basic membership at Rand McNally includes multi-stop road trips, and comes free of charge.

4 Once registered, click **Plan a Road Trip** to specify the route, beginning with the name of your trip.

104

Plan a road trip

Enter the details for your road trip.

1. Enter the starting point address, or just city and state.

2. Put the destination point details next.

3. Optionally provide starting and ending dates for your trip.

4. For a roundtrip, it creates the return route for you.

5. Click **Continue**, and the trip so far is displayed.

6. Click **Add a Stop** and enter the address and optionally the arrival date for a stopover point.

7. Click **Continue**, and add any further stopover points required.

Hot tip

If the address is not completely defined, you may see a list of possible locations from which you can choose.

Don't forget

If the route suggested is not exactly what you want, you could introduce an extra stopover, e.g. you might add Lillooet between Whistler and Kamloops.

Print trip guide

When you have completed the route you can save it. Up to ten such routes can be saved at the website. You can view, edit or print the saved trips whenever you wish.

1. When you print the route, add "Step-by-Step directions".

2. You can also add weather data for each of the stop points.

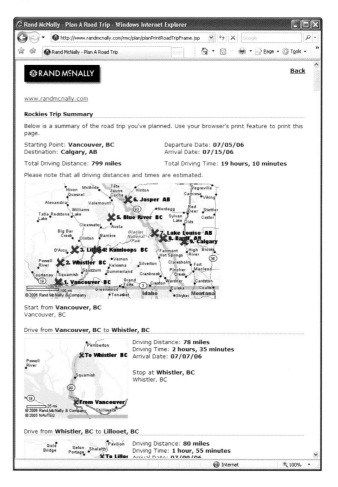

(8) Explore your Family Tree

The Internet has created a whole new way to search for information on your family background and your ancestors. You can share information with other parts of the same family, without having to travel around, even if your ancestral roots are from far distant shores.

Don't forget

Other equivalent terms are ancestry, forebears, descent, lineage and pedigree, though that last term is usually associated with non-human groupings.

Beware

Genealogy research can turn into an obsession, as you reach further back in time, to solve puzzles and discover facts that others have missed.

Hot tip

You can download versions of these forms to print and complete manually, or to fill out using your computer software (see details on page 111).

Introduction to genealogy

The term Genealogy applies to the study of the history of past and present members of a particular family. It also applies to the records and documentation that describe that history, the members of the family and their relationships.

Genealogy is highly popular right across the world. There are many reasons why you might research your family's history:

- Simple curiosity about yourself and your roots
- Make your children aware of their ancestors
- Preserve family cultural and ethnic traditions
- Medical family history (inherited disease or attribute)
- Join a lineage or heritage society

Getting started is generally quite easy – you find the oldest living members of your family and ask them about other members, especially those who are no longer here to answer for themselves.

After the first flush of success however, it could become difficult to fill in the gaps and extend the history further back in time. You have to rely on official records, and this could require a lot of travel, especially if your family originated overseas. Fortunately, much of the necessary legwork can now be accomplished over the Internet, there's plenty of advice and guidance, and you'll be able to capitalize on the research that others have carried out.

The information you glean can be recorded on charts designed to organize genealogical data.

- Ascendant, Ahnentafel and Pedigree charts
- Descendant, Progenitor charts
- Family Group sheets

These forms and the way to use them are described in various tutorials (see page 109).

Researching your family tree

If you are new to genealogy, perhaps the best place to start is with an online (and free) genealogy tutorial.

1 There's a tutorial "Researching Your Family Tree" at **www.lcarnwcbskills.com/family/intro.html** which provides a self-paced introduction.

Follow the modules in this tutorial to research your own ancestors while learning to use the genealogical charts, online databases and other resources.

2 You can communicate with other users of the tutorial through the Yahoo group **Learngen**. The tutorial includes instructions for joining this group.

Hot tip

Search Google for "Genealogy Tutorial" (the quotes mean the exact phrase), and you get 2110 matching web pages.

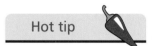

Hot tip

The navigation bar on the left lists the contents of the six modules, plus more than 20 useful website links.

Don't forget

The Tools section has links to charts and tools (see page 111).

Tools

Home Sources Checklist
5-Generation Ancestor Chart
4-Generation Ancestor Chart
Family Group Sheet
Birth Date Calculator
Town to County Database

Genealogy 101

① For a somewhat more structured introduction, go to **genealogy.about.com** and click **Genealogy 101**.

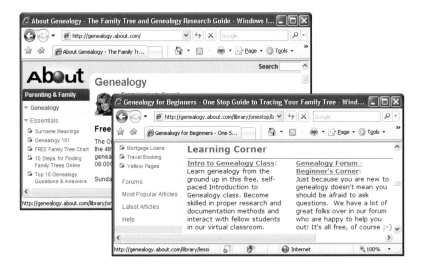

② Scroll down to the **Learning Corner** and click the **Intro to Genealogy Class** link.

This class currently consists of four lessons:
- Genealogical Basics
- Family & Home Sources
- Genealogy Research 101
- Vital Records – Birth, Marriage, Divorce, Death

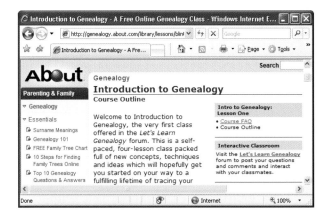

Genealogy charts

1 Go to **www.ancestry.com** (a site suggested by both tutorials) and click the **Family Trees** button.

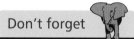

Don't forget

Most genealogy websites will have free charts available. There are also many commercial products on offer.

2 Scroll down the **Family Tree Resources** and then click the **Print a Family Tree Chart** entry.

Don't forget

You may need to install the Adobe Reader to view and print the charts (see page 74).

111

3 Click **Download Form** to view or print the PDF form in your browser, or right-click and select **Save Target As...** to save the file on your hard disk.

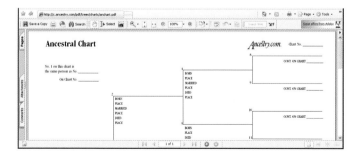

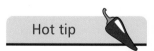
Hot tip

The Ancestry.com family tree resources also include a family group form, census forms for the US, UK and Canada, and other record forms.

Charts in text format

If you want to complete your genealogy forms on your computer, you need the forms in a text format.

1 At the Family Tree website **www.familytreemagazine.com**, click the **free research forms** link found in the Tool Kit.

Download Forms
Free research forms, ancestor charts, census forms and more!

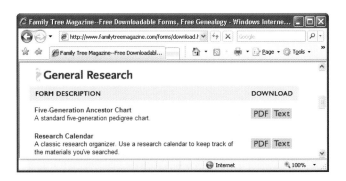

2 This displays the Forms Download area, where you will find PDF and Word versions of the charts.

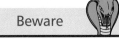

Vital records

When you've collected all the information you can from family members, and organized it using genealogy charts, you'll have a list of unanswered questions, and you'll need to start searching records to find some of the answers.

There are two main types of genealogical records that you can investigate:

Original records

An original record is an account of a specific event, written at or near the time the event took place. Historically, many civil and religious authorities kept records on events in the lives of people in their jurisdictions. Original records include:

- Vital Records (birth, marriage, divorce and death)
- Church Records (christenings, baptisms, confirmations, marriages, or burials)
- Cemetery Records (names, dates, and relationships)
- Census Records (household member name, sex, age, country or state of birth, occupation)
- Military, Probate, Immigration Records

Compiled records

A compiled record is a collection of information on a specific person, family group or topic. Compiled records exist because others have already researched original records or collated information from other compiled records or other sources. Compiled records include:

- Ancestral File (over 13 million names, linked into ancestors and descendants)
- International Genealogical Index (computerized index of over 187 million names extracted from birth, christening, marriage, and other records)
- Published Family Histories, Biographies, Genealogies, and Local Histories

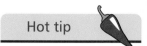

Hot tip

You may be able to access original records on microfiche, and some, especially census records, have been indexed and computerized. See page 116.

Don't forget

Compiled records are useful if you want to learn about ancestors who were born before 1900, but are not likely to have information about modern families.

113

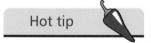

Hot tip

The two main compiled record files were developed by the family history department of the Church of Latter-Day Saints (see page 115).

Cyndi's List

To find out where to look for original records, you should start at **www.cyndislist.com,** a search engine that is dedicated to genealogical research via the internet. You can search for helpful websites by location or by record type.

1 Click Beginners in the main category index, and you'll be able to view lists of websites related to researching various types of original and vital records.

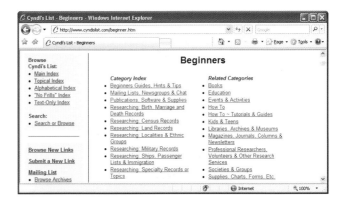

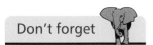
2 **Researching: Census Records** gives lists of USA and worldwide census sites, plus details on Soundex indexing.

FamilySearch

The **www.familysearch.org** website owned and operated by the Church of Latter-day Saints provides free family history.

115

Don't forget

Advanced Search lets you add parent and spouse names for a particular ancestor.

1 The minimum information you need provide is the surname. The exact spelling isn't essential.

2 Select a record type (life event) for which you have the year (exact, or give or take 2, 5, 10 or 20 years).

Birth/Christening
All
Birth/Christening
Marriage
Death/Burial
Other

3 Choose the country, and (for Canada and the US) the state.

Hot tip

The records found will provide you with further clues about the person and family, perhaps including, as in this case, a pedigree chart, with links back to further charts.

4 Matching records are displayed. Review the records, to confirm you have identified the correct person.

Pedigree Chart

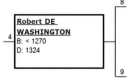

Ancestry.com

You can search for ancestors at **www.ancestry.com**. This website has many databases, including census, birth, marriage, death, military and immigration. It offers paid membership subscriptions, but there is a free Registered Guest account, which allows you to receive the free newsletter and build an online family tree, and access some of the databases.

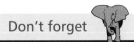

Don't forget

If you are interested in Canadian data, evaluate Ancestry.ca instead. For United Kingdom data, try Ancestry.co.uk.

Beware

The Guest membership is well hidden, so you need to issue a search to find the details.

 At **www.ancestry.com**, select Help and type **Guest** in the Search box then click the Search button.

Select the article **Ancestry Registered Guest Account** for details, and select Click Here to sign up.

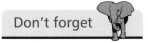

Don't forget

You'll receive two emails. In the first, simply click to confirm your request. The second email has your account details.

Register your name and email ID, and you will be sent a confirmatory email and your guest user name and password.

3 Sign on using your guest user name and password.

4 Search for one of your ancestors, giving all the details that you have available, and selecting a Ranked Search.

5 You'll see a list of matching records, and some of the details will be revealed. You can narrow the search to see which specific databases contain relevant data.

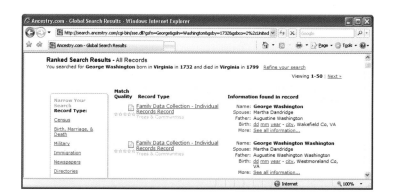

6 You can view details in the free databases, but when you try to obtain details from a members-only database, you'll be invited to sign up for the 14 day free trial.

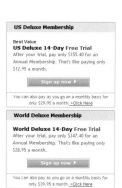

7 Decide whether you need data for US only or Worldwide. There's an equivalent choice for the Canada and UK sites.

8 Choose between annual payment and monthly payment (and pay per view, in Canada and UK).

Don't forget

The guest account allows you to explore the databases, without having to use up the time on your 14 day free trial until you are ready to proceed in earnest.

Don't forget

If it is just Canadian data you need, look at Ancestry.ca. For United Kingdom data, look at Ancestry.co.uk. You can sign on at either website using your Ancestry.com guest account.

Ancestry.ca
Ancestry.co.uk

Beware

The green button means an annual commitment. It is the >Click Here link that enrols you into monthly membership.

117

US National Archives

Some of the answers to your questions may be found in the US National Archives at the website **www.archives.gov**.

1 Select the **Genealogists/Family Historians** link where you'll find help and guidance to get started.

2 Select **Forms, Tools & Aids** and click **Order Online** for information on obtaining copies of records.

Now you can order certain genealogical records online through <u>Order Online</u>!

3 You may have to visit in person for some of your research (or hire an independent researcher to work on your behalf).

Other National Archives

Other countries will of course have their own equivalent to the US National Archives. For Australian information, go to **www.naa.gov.au**, and click **Getting Started** for more details.

Don't forget

Any person is entitled to visit the archives and use its services. You don't need to be an Australian citizen or resident.

You'd visit **www.collectionscanada.ca/index-e.html** for Canadian records (or **/index-f.html** for the French version).

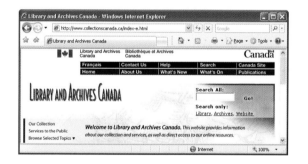

Hot tip

There's a link to the Canadian Genealogy Center, which offers genealogical content, services, advice and research tools.

The UK has its records at **www.nationalarchives.gov.uk**.

Hot tip

The UK site has an explicit Family History section with expert advice on using the archives to build up your family tree.

Immigrant records

If your family origins are from overseas, you will need to find the connection between the two family groups. Immigration records may be the answer.

The website **www.immigrantships.net** makes passenger lists available for a number of ships, though it is important to remember that it was 1820 before the federal government began requiring passenger lists from ship captains.

Don't forget

You'll find immigrant records for earlier dates in the US immigration databases at Genealogy.com

John Washington found in:
Passenger and Immigration Index, 1500s-1900s
🛈 More Information

Hot tip

Castle Garden was the landing port before Ellis Island, for 1851-1891. Records for this period are found in Genealogy.com.

Ellis Island, just off Manhattan Island, New York, became the gateway to the United States from 1892 to 1924, during which time over 20 million immigrants passed through the immigration station. The website is **www.ellisisland.org**.

9 Digital Photography

Find advice and guidance on the Internet to improve your skill and technique. Store and backup your digital photographs and print online photos. Share your photos with your friends and family, and view the results obtained using various cameras and lenses.

Tips on the Internet

If you use a digital camera, the Internet becomes a natural extension. It offers a wide range of digital photographic information, facilities and tools. These may be provided by institutions such as colleges and libraries, equipment manufacturers, individuals, enthusiasts or professional photographers.

To start with, there are websites that tell you how to improve your digital photography skills and techniques.

Don't forget

The camera and equipment suppliers are keen to encourage you to develop your skills. They are worth visiting, even if you favor a different make of camera.

 Fuji has some tips for better photographs and a useful glossary, at **www.fujifilm.com/support**.

Don't forget

Digital Photography is covered in-depth in another title from this series called Digital Photography for Seniors in Easy Steps.

There's a rather more comprehensive website offered by Kodak. Go to **www.kodak.com** and click **Consumer Photography** and then **Taking Great Pictures**.

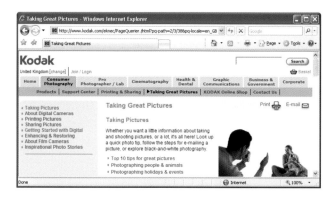

Hot tip

Most of the tips for taking pictures apply equally to digital and film photography.

Review the tips in the **Taking Pictures** section, or select **Getting Started with Digital**.

Tutorials

There are numerous tutorials on various aspects of digital photography, some for beginners, for example those at the ShortCourses website:

 Switch to **www.shortcourses.com/editing** for a short course on editing digital photographs.

Hot tip

Click the Home button to see the full list of the short courses that are on offer.

 If you are ready for a challenge, view the tutorial **Making fine prints in your digital darkroom**, at the **www.normankoren.com** website.

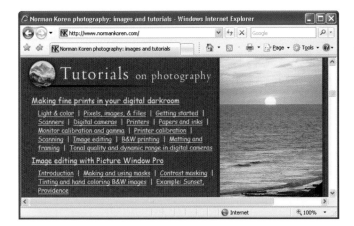

Don't forget

This is a multi-part series that introduces tools and techniques for making fine prints digitally, to meet the highest aesthetic and technical standards.

Find inspiration

Digital photography is not just about equipment and techniques, it is also about subject and composition. Perhaps the best way to explore these aspects is through viewing the work of other photographers, for example at the Photographic Society of America.

The Society awards EPSA (Excellence in Photography) and PPSA (Proficiency in Photography), based on achievements in photography exhibitions.

1 At **www.psa-photo.org/page2.htm**, select one of the galleries and choose members by name to view examples of their work, such as illustrated here.

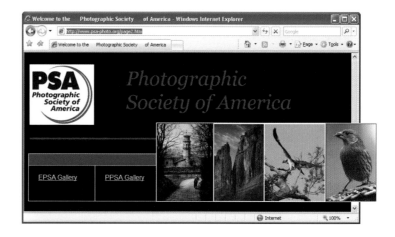

2 The Royal Photographic Society allows members to upload their portfolios to the Society website. They can be viewed at **www.rps.org/portfolios.php**

You do not need to be a member to view the portfolios. However, if you do join, you'll find that the RPS has a special interest group for Digital Imaging.

Share photos online

You can use the Internet to share your digital photographs. You don't have to join a society and create a portfolio, and the photographs can be private, just for friends and family.

Hot tip

Kodak runs Ofoto so the address becomes www.kodakgallery.com and you can use either address to visit the website.

1 Visit the website **www.ofoto.com** and click the **Get Started** button.

2 Provide your first name, email ID, password, your cell phone number (optional). No credit card is needed. Click the **Create Account** button.

3 Your gallery is assigned, and a confirming email is sent to the email ID you provided.

Don't forget

If you are located outside the US, click the Change link and select your country before registering, to get local prices and shipping charges.

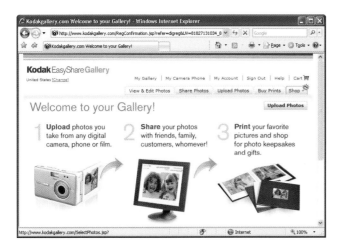

4 You are now ready to upload photographs.

Upload photographs

1 Click the **Upload Photos** button to create a new album.

Hot tip

You might find it more useful to put the date you took the photos, rather than the date you created the album.

2 Provide album name, create date, brief description, use filename, and click **Continue**.

3 Choose to install the **Easy Upload** software, and follow the installation prompts as provided.

4 Click **Add Pictures** and choose images (.jpg file format only) from your photo folder.

Don't forget

Easy Upload allows you to select ranges of files at a time, e.g. click the first image, hold down Shift, then click the last image.

5 Click **Add More Pictures**, if there is another folder to transfer, then click on **Start Upload**.

6 Thumbnails are dropped from the holding area as each image is transferred. There's also a progress bar.

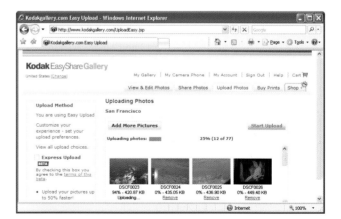

Beware

If your images are saved in a format other than .jpg, you must use an image editing application to convert the files, before you upload.

7 When the upload completes, carry on with the next action e.g. upload another folder.

✓ 77 photos have been uploaded to this album.
Do more: Share Album | Buy Prints | Upload more photos

View albums

1 Sign in to Kodak Gallery (or click **My Gallery** if you are already signed in) to list your albums.

2 Click an album to display thumbnails of its contents.

3 Click **Edit Details & Rearrange** to make changes, or click **Slideshow** to view the photos in turn.

4 Click any thumbnail to jump to that position.

Click the Options link below a thumbnail and select View Larger, to edit the photo title, or make changes to the image.

Don't forget

You can edit the images before printing them (see page 130).

Share albums

You can invite your friends and family to view your digital photographs, by sending them an email.

1 Click the Share Photos tab and choose an album, then click the Select Album button.

2 The album is added to the list of albums that are available for sharing.

3 When you've added all the albums you want to share at this time, click the **Continue** button.

4 Enter the email address and amend the message if desired, then click the **Send Invitation** button.

5 Your friends click the **View photos** link in their email, and sign in.

View friends' albums

If your friends upload digital photographs, they can invite you to share their albums, by sending you an email.

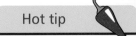

Hot tip

When you receive invitations to view slideshows, you will have the ability to share their photos with other friends and family.

 Click the **View Photos** link in your email, and sign in to view their slideshows.

When you click **Exit Slideshow**, their albums are added to your gallery, in a separate Friends area.

Don't forget

You can treat the shared photos just like your own and purchase prints or create a picture mug etc. (see page 130).

Hover the mouse pointer over a shared album, to see your friend's name and the album title.

Order prints

Kodak provides a printing service, which is their motivation for providing storage on the Internet. They keep the original image file (even though slideshows use reduced images) so prints will be full quality.

1. Sign in and click **My Gallery,** open an album and click **Buy Prints,** then select photos to print.

2. When you've finished choosing, click **Add to Cart**.

3. You can specify photos individually, or choose the Express options for all the photos in the order.

4 Click **Checkout** to specify shipping and payment.

Hot tip

You can arrange to pick up your order at a retail store. You'll pay a $1.49 fee, but no shipping charge. This applies to US website accounts only.

Select In-Store Pickup Location

Add Pickup Location

5 Provide the delivery address details (this could be your own or a friend's address).

Enter Shipping Address

First Name:*
Senior

Last Name:*
Ies

Address 1:*

Primary street or P.O. Box

6 Make this the default address, if appropriate, then click the **Save** button.

☑ Make this my default shipping address.
Save

7 The rates depend on the order size and on the shipping speed that you request.

Choose a shipping speed:
◉ 3-7 Day delivery after processing* ($1.49)
○ 2-Day delivery after processing* ($10.99)
○ 1-Day delivery after processing* ($15.99)

phone:
2-day and 1-day deliveries require a phone number.

Beware

You will be charged prices and shipping based on the website where you register (see page 125). If you are UK based, but have a US account, you'll pay international shipping.

Choose a shipping speed:
◉ Air 1st Class $4.99
○ Air Express $19.99
○ 1-Day delivery after pro

8 Click **Next** to check the order summary and then add your credit card details, before you click **Place Order** to complete your purchase.

cart shipping summary payment
Add another recipient **Next ▶**

131

Storage and backup

The EasyShare Gallery provides free, unlimited online photo storage for 12 months from the date of your first upload, and will store the photos online for as long as your account is active. That means making at least one purchase from the Gallery every 12 months.

You can preserve your entire photo collection on disc with Archive CDs. These contain a separate file for each photo, at the resolution in which it was uploaded.

Don't forget

The cost of archive CDs depends on how many photographs you have in your albums.

Pricing

Archive CDs are priced according to the total number of photos in your account.

1-50 photos	$9.95
51-100 photos	$14.95
101-250 photos	$19.95
251-500 photos	$29.95
501-1000 photos	$39.95
Each additional 1,000	$14.95

Beware

There is no premier subscription or archive CD facility available at the international EasyShare websites.

132

① Click the **Shop** tab, then click the **Archive CDs** entry in the Shop For list.

② Gallery Premier provides a personal homepage, and also maintains your photo storage (without further purchases) while the subscription is in effect.

Yahoo photos

There are other websites that offer free, unlimited online photo storage, Yahoo Photos for example. This does not have a purchase requirement, but you do need a Yahoo ID to sign up (see page 137 to create a free Yahoo ID).

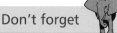

Yahoo! Photos
Share your joy with photo books and custom gifts. Get started

1 Go to **www.yahoo.com** and click on **Yahoo Photos**.

2 Sign in to Yahoo using your existing ID and password.

3 Your Yahoo ID is now associated with Yahoo Photos.

4 Click **Create New Album** to start adding photos.

To access Yahoo! Photos...
Sign in to Yahoo!

Yahoo! ID: senior_ies
Password: ••••••••

☐ Remember my ID on this computer

Sign In

Why this is secure

Forget your ID or password?
Sign-in help

Don't have a Yahoo! ID?
Signing up is easy.

Sign Up

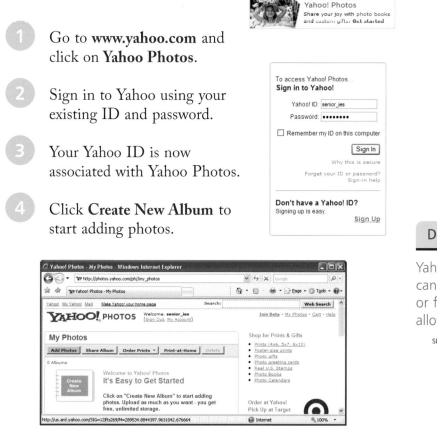

Don't forget

Yahoo photo albums can be private, public or friends only (a list of allowed Yahoo users).

Sharing Setting

⦿ 🔒 **Private**
Only those you invite by email

○ 🌐 **Public**
Everyone can view this album

○ 👥 **Friends Only**
Only Yahoo! users listed below

133

5 Provide an album name (including the create date), select the share setting and click the **Continue** button.

6 Click the **Get Started** button and follow the instructions to install the Easy Update tool, which allows you to drag and drop photos into the photo album.

Hot tip

It is not essential to install the Yahoo toolbar when you install the Easy Update software.

PBase Galleries

The PBase photo sharing and hosting site encourages public viewing, giving serious photographers the opportunity to display their skills to the world. You'll usually find information on the settings and equipment used, and lots of comments made by other viewers.

1 The PBase website is at **www.pbase.com**. Click **Popular Galleries** to view slideshows, or click the **Search** button to look for particular subjects.

2 For example, a search for **Auroras** produced several pages of fascinating Northern Lights slideshows.

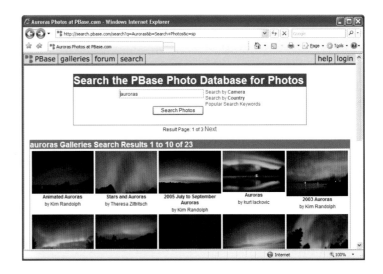

10 Keep in Touch

Whether you are at home, or on vacation, the Internet helps you to keep in touch with your family and friends. You can send and receive email, exchange instant messages or send electronic greetings.

Email communication

The Internet allows you to communicate with friends, family and business contacts quickly and easily, whether they are just down the street or on the other side of the world. You can send to individuals, or whole groups of people such as club members, with a simple click of the mouse button. You can include photographs with your email and attach all kinds of documents such as Minutes, Agendas and Reports.

Email requires two things – software that allows you to create, save, send and receive messages and an Internet connection.

The Software

Microsoft's Outlook and Outlook Express can both be used for email. They are programs that come with Windows. Outlook is a full Personal Information Manager which includes an email program. Outlook Express is a subset of Oulook which is just the email element.

However, many Internet Service Providers offer their own email facility. They allow you to create, send, receive, read and store your email on their server, using your browser. This is known as Webmail or sometimes Netmail. Its big advantage is that you can access your mail from anywhere in the world – from a friend's PC, an hotel or Internet cafe. It does, however, mean that you must be online when using it.

Web-based email

Each individual ISP offers their own mailbox structure, but they are all very similar in approach. If you are accustomed to using Outlook Express, you will find the transition to a web-based facility very straightforward.

Some email accounts are normally web-based only, for example Hotmail and Yahoo. For the purposes of this book, we will be using Yahoo mail.

Don't forget

If you have a dial-up connection, you may prefer to use Outlook or Outlook Express at home as they allow you to compose and read your messages off-line, without paying for connection time. Email using Outlook and Outlook Express is covered in-depth in Computing for Seniors in Easy Steps.

Hot tip

When setting up your email account, check to see if your ISP allows Webmail, especially if you anticipate travelling and want to be able to keep in touch.

Create a webmail account

Your ISP may already provide you with a webmail account. However, if you need a new account, you can create one at Yahoo.com:

 Start Internet Explorer, go to **www.yahoo.com** and click on the **Mail** icon.

Read and click OK on the security alert. Then select **Sign Up**.

> Don't have a Yahoo! ID?
> Signing up is easy.
>
> **Sign Up**

Complete all the required fields (those marked with an asterisk), type in your preferred choice of ID and click **Check Availability**.

Complete and verify registration details, then check and agree to the terms and conditions.

Create Your Yahoo! ID

* First name:	Sue
* Last name:	Price
* Preferred content:	Yahoo! U.S.
* Gender:	Female
* Yahoo! ID:	senior_ies @yahoo.com

ID may consist of a-z, 0-9, underscores, and a single dot (.)

Check Availability of This ID

You will then be able to select marketing, subscription and third party options. It's a good idea to keep these to a minimum initially. When you have finished the process remember to Log out.

The new account can be used to register for other Yahoo services such as Yahoo Photos (see page 133).

Hot tip

With so many people now using email, you may find that your preferred name has already been taken. If so, Yahoo helps by asking you to type in three words, from which they will suggest a suitable ID for you.

Enter up to **three words** for some available ID suggestions:
(recommended)

1.	senior
2.	internet
3.	easy steps

Example: a favorite place, pet, and color

Show Some IDs

137

Don't forget

The verification process is used to prevent automated registrations. You must be able to read the monitor to type in the letters – something that can only be achieved with the human eye.

The webmail window

With your mail account now set up, connect to Yahoo.com and sign in.

Beware

The Yahoo mail sign-in screen offers the option to remember your password. This is fine in a domestic situation, but do not select it on anyone else's PC or in an Internet cafe. See also page 173 (delete browsing history).

The Welcome screen has four main tabs:

- Mail (currently selected) shows the standard folder structure and number of new messages waiting

- Addresses gives you access to your Address Book

- Calendar is a diary function

- Notes is a small memo function

The folders within the Mail Box are where your messages are stored, and will allow you to organize your mail

- the Inbox is where your mail arrives. To view your new mail, click on the Inbox folder

- Drafts is where you will store any incomplete messages, or one that you do not want to send immediately

- the Sent folder keeps a copy of email sent

- the Bulk folder will contain any messages that the Yahoo spamguard program isolates as unwanted

- Trash contains any messages that are no longer required

Don't forget

Spam is the term applied to unwanted, unsolicited and inappropriate messages. Yahoo provides a Spamguard program to scan email for such messages, and it is automatically switched on when you sign up with a new ID.

Access your mail

[Screenshot of Yahoo! Mail Inbox in Windows Internet Explorer]

Hot tip

Click the checkbox next to each message in the Inbox to select it. You can select multiple messages and then click Delete, Spam etc.

① Click on **Check Mail** or the Inbox folder in the left panel to show new messages. The number (3) indicates that there are three new messages.

② Click on the message subject to open the message. The message header indicates the date and sender.

③ With the message open, select from the options to Delete, Reply, Forward, mark as Spam or move to another folder. Alternatively, you can select **Next** or **Previous** (message).

[Screenshot showing message view with "Hooray! Your first email."]

Don't forget

The messages will remain in the Inbox unless you Delete, mark as Spam or Move to another folder.

④ Click **Back to Messages** to return to the Inbox view.

Create and send mail

1 Click **Compose** on the Inbox window to create a new message.

2 Select the recipient, either by typing their address, or by clicking on **Insert Addresses** to add addresses from your Address Book.

3 Press the Tab key or click in the Subject box and type in the topic of the email.

Don't forget

You can insert the address for more than one recipient and can also send Carbon Copies (CCs) and Blind Carbon Copies (BCCs).

Don't forget
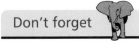

Use Save as Draft for unfinished email messages, or to delay sending.

Yahoo! Mail - senior_ies@yahoo.com - Windows Internet Explorer

Mail ▾ Addresses ▾ Calendar ▾ Notepad ▾   What's New - Upgrades - Options

Send   Save as a Draft   Cancel   Send an eCard

Insert addresses | Add CC - Add BCC

To: jesmith@dial.pipex.com

Subject: U3A Bridge session

Attach Files

Stationery

Hi Jes
Just to let you know that we have sufficient numbers signed up for the session to make up 24 tables. I will be in touch later with a list of names.

We must get together with Jill to plan refreshments.

☐ Use my signature

Send   Save as a Draft   Cancel

🌐 Internet   🔍 100% ▾

4 Tab again to the message area which offers standard word processing tools, such as different font styles and spell checking. Type your message and click **Send**. You will get confirmation that the email has been sent.

5 Click **Back to Inbox** to continue with messaging activities.

Hot tip

Click Add to Address Book to add any new email addresses that you have used.

Message Sent

Sent to:
jessmith@dial.pipex.com   ✔

Add to Address Book

Back to Inbox

Manage your mail

Webmail ISPs allocate you storage space on their server when you sign up for their email facility. Yahoo for example, gives you 1Gb of storage, which depending on your level of activity, should be ample for most people.

Sort your messages

 Click in the header area on Sender or Subject to sort alphabetically, click again to sort in reverse order.

 Click **Date** to sort your messages newest to oldest or again to sort in reverse order.

Delete	Spam	Mark ▼	Move... ▼		
☐ Sender		Subject		Date ▣	Size
☐ Yahoo!		Welcome to Yahoo!		Sat Jul 01, 2006	524b
☑ MAILER-DAEMON@yahoo.com		failure notice		Sun Jul 02, 2006	4k

Select your messages

 Click in the box to the left of the message to select it (insert a tick). Click again if you wish to remove the tick. You can tick as many messages at a time as you wish.

Folders	[Add - Edit]		View: All Messages ▼		Messages 1-6 of 6
📁 Inbox (3)			Delete	Spam	Mark ▼	Move... ▼
📁 Draft			☐ Sender		Subject
📁 Sent			☑ MAILER-DAEMON@yahoo.com		failure notice
📁 Bulk	[Empty]		☑ maprice@dial.pipex.com		View my photos
📁 Trash	[Empty]				
My Folders	[Hide]				

Delete your messages

 Click **Delete** to transfer all selected messages to the Trash folder. Messages in the Trash folder do not count towards your total storage.

Hot tip

Tick the box next to Sender to select or deselect all messages.

Don't forget

Messages will remain in the Trash folder, allowing you to reinstate them if necessary. Click on Empty to empty the Trash folder.

Create and use folders

To create folders for webmail storage:

 Select one or more messages with a check mark and click the **Move** button.

 Click **New Folder**.
If you have Pop-ups blocked, see page 172, you will have to temporarily allow them and repeat steps one and two.

see page 172

Don't forget

You are only allowed to use letters, numbers, underscores and hyphens in folder names.

Name the folder and click OK. The new folder will appear in the folder list under the subheading **My Folders**.

The next time you click the **Move** button, you will have the option to move selected items to the new folder.

Hot tip

You can Hide or Show your list of My Folders.

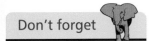

Don't forget

Use this view of the folders to monitor your storage situation.

To rename or delete a folder, click on **Edit** at the top of the Folder list. You will see a full list of folder contents including the size. Select an action for the relevant folder by clicking on the option in square brackets under the folder name.

Folders   [Add - Edit]

  Inbox (3)
  Draft
  Sent
  Bulk   [Empty]
  Trash   [Empty]

My Folders   [Hide]
  U3A

Folders

Name	Messages	Unread	Size
Inbox	6	3	53k
Draft	1	1	0k
Sent	1	0	2k
[Options]			
Bulk	0	0	---
[Empty - Options]			
Trash	0	0	---
[Empty]			
U3A	0	0	0k
[Rename - Delete]			
Total	8	4	55k

Webmail options

Customize your webmail account and take advantage of features offered by your ISP, using Options on the main Mail window.

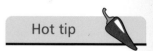

Spam

SpamGuard is on when you sign up to Yahoo. Click on Spam Protection to change settings, such as how long to keep spam messages, where to move allowed messages and how to handle spam images.

Blocked Addresses

This function allows you to block messages from your Inbox for up to 500 addresses or domain names. The blocked messages will be deleted before you see them.

Filters

Filters are applied to your incoming mail. You can use filters to automatically sort your mail into appropriate folders. Click on Filters, and then Add. You can choose details within the Header, To box, From box, Subject and body of message.

Hot tip

Other webmail options include adding an automatic signature, setting an auto response when you are away or on vacation and setting your general preferences.

143

Don't forget

Webmail providers will also offer more sophisticated functions, improved filters, larger amounts of storage etc. on a chargeable basis.

Attachments

You can attach documents and photos to your email with a webmail account.

1 Create your email in the usual way and click the button to **Attach Files**.

2 Click **Browse** and navigate your PC's folders to locate and select the required file. Click Open. Repeat to attach more files.

3 Click the **Attach Files** button. The file(s) will be checked for viruses. Click **Continue to Message** to complete your email and then send.

Receive attachments

When you receive a file with an attachment:

1 Check that you know the sender. If you are unsure of the source, then be on your guard.

2 Open the message, the attachment will be shown, in this instance, at the bottom of the message.

3 Click on the file name, or on **Scan and Save to Computer**.

Beware

You should always scan attachments for viruses, even if you do know the sender. Yahoo webmail provides a virus scanner. Check your provider to see what it offers.

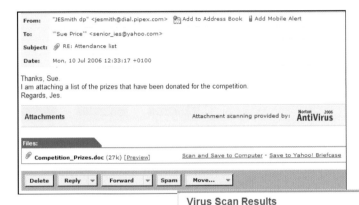

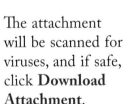

4 The attachment will be scanned for viruses, and if safe, click **Download Attachment**.

Virus Scan Results

File name:	Competition_Prizes.doc
File size:	27kb
File type:	application/msword
Scan result:	No virus threat detected.

Scanned with: Norton AntiVirus 2006   Keep your computer safe from [...] the Symantec Security Connecti[...]

[Download Attachment] [Back to Message]

5 You will have a further opportunity to Open or Save the attachment. Normally you would select **Save** and then choose the appropriate folder.

Don't forget

You may need to select a new destination folder as the computer will remember the previous destination of a downloaded file and will open that folder automatically.

145

E-cards

You can send all kinds of free greeting cards to friends and family using the Internet. Yahoo, for example, provides e-cards which you can access using your Yahoo ID.

1 Log in to Yahoo Mail and click **Compose**. Click the button to Send an e-Card.

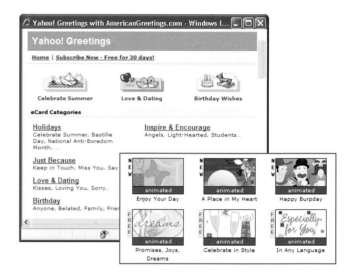

2 Choose a category and select a card from the illustrations. Free cards and animated cards will be labeled.

E-postcards

Many tourist destinations have comprehensive websites, to advertise facilities, activities, hotels etc. Check these sites for digital postcards – a good way to stay in touch when traveling.

Instant messaging

Many ISPs and other software companies provide Instant Messaging services. This service allows you to communicate with a selected list of contacts, either by typing your message, or by voice. With a camera attached to your PC, some instant messaging programs will even allow you to transmit (and receive) video.

For this you will need to download and install special software. In this example we shall use Skype, which is available at no charge and provides full video service.

Don't forget

You will need a full DSL (broadband) service to use Instant Messaging.

 Visit **www.skype.com** and click the Download now button.

Save the file to a Downloads folder or to the Desktop. When the download is complete, open the folder and double-click the file to start the installation.

Follow the on-screen instructions to choose the program location and other options. It is usually best to accept the defaults.

Beware

Skype's on-screen instructions suggest that when you have downloaded the file you select to Run it. Their help page suggests you save it to the Desktop and Run later, a better option.

Sign up to Skype

When you start Skype for the first time you will need to sign in and create an identity for yourself.

1 Open Skype and click Don't have a Skype Name. Supply a User name and password. As with the Yahoo ID, you may need to try several different names to find one available.

2 On the next step, follow the on-screen instructions and fill in as many details as you wish to **Help your friends find you**.

3 There is then a tutorial on how to get started with Skype, the final step of which will allow Skype to check through Address Books on your PC to identify friends who already have a Skype identity. Tick those names you wish to add to your Skype list of contacts.

Add more contacts

Skype selects from your Address Book those addresses it recognizes as having access to Skype. However, you may wish to add other names from your Address Book.

1 In the main Skype window click Tools, **Share Skype with a friend**.

2 Complete the form with your own and the friend's details and click **Send This**. Your friend will receive an email to join, with an option to download the Skype program.

Delete	Spam	Mark ▼	Move... ▼
☐ **Sender**		**Subject**	
☐ Skype		Have you got the new Skype?	

3 As an alternative, just click **Add a Contact** in the main window, enter a new contact's details and let Skype search for the contact.

4 Whichever way you add your contacts, you will need to get a confirming response from them that they are happy to join your instant messaging community. The agreement of course works both ways – you will be asked if you wish to join their contact list.

Don't forget

You can use Skype to phone landline and mobile phone numbers, but you will need to purchase credit from Skype to use the facility.

Make a call

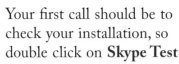

Your first call should be to check your installation, so double click on **Skype Test Call**. You will hear a voice asking you to record a ten second message which will be played back to you if your system is working correctly.

To connect with a friend, double click their name or select their name and click on the green phone.

You will hear a ringing tone. If they are online they will be informed that you are calling. If they are offline, you will be informed.

You can type your messages or with a microphone attached to your PC you will be able to have live conversations. With a video camera attached, click the **Start My Video** button to show your own image nested inside a larger video of your contact.

Click the **History** tab to see a record of all calls to and from your PC, including those missed.

11 Publish to the Internet

Become completely involved in the Internet phenomena by creating your own website, and let other web users visit your web pages. If you've got something to say, but don't want a complete website perhaps you could try your hand at blogging (writing a web log), or access feeds to stay up to the minute with website changes.

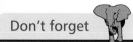

Build a web page

If you have something to share, why not create your own page on the web? Think of things you might want to publish in your web page. It doesn't have to be for business. It could be just for fun, so you can learn first hand about the way the Internet operates. It might be a place where you store information related to a hobby or interest, that you'd like to share with others who have the same interests. You might have project reports, how-to guides, book reports, photographs or links to associated web pages.

Whatever you want to put in your web page, you will need three main items:

1 Storage space on the Internet to record the text and images that you want to share.

2 Tools and facilities to help you assemble and arrange those components into the form of a web page.

3 An Internet address that you can give to others so that they can view your web page.

Your Internet Service Provider may make web space available as part of your Internet account, and provide the addressing needed. They would also provide or recommend suitable tools and techniques for building and publishing your web page. However, often the ISP facilities are limited to a predefined home page that may limit what you are able to achieve. Creating your web page at the ISP would also make it harder for you to switch suppliers, if your requirements were to change.

Fortunately, there are many other Internet services that will meet all of the requirements for building web pages. For some, it is their main business and they will require a monthly or annual fee, except perhaps for the initial trial period. Others, such as Yahoo are already providing services and offer web page creation as an additional free feature.

Yahoo and GeoCities

The web building services offered by Yahoo are under the GeoCities label. You'll find a link at the Yahoo website, or you can go straight to GeoCities.

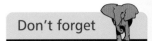

Don't forget

You use the same Yahoo ID to sign in to any of the Yahoo services, including web-mail, photos, groups and geocities.

1 Go to the website **geocities.yahoo.com**, and click the **Sign Up Now** button.

2 All you need to access GeoCities is your Yahoo ID and password. Enter these and click **Sign In**.

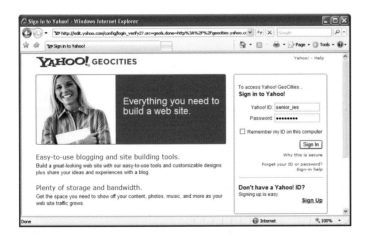

3 If you have not yet obtained your Yahoo ID, click **Sign Up** to enroll (see page 137).

153

Verify registration

You are asked to complete a small survey, indicating the type of website you plan to build, and where you learned about the GeoCities free service.

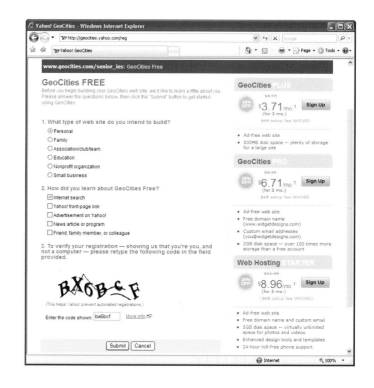

Beware

Case is not important for the picture code, but you must enter the correct letters and numbers. This is a security measure to avoid attempts to create multiple IDs using a computer program.

Click the buttons for your answers to the questions, type in the pictorial code, and click **Submit**.

Hot tip

You'll also receive an email with these details, and advice on getting started with your web page.

Your home page will be **www.geocities.com/your_id**, where **your_id** is your Yahoo ID (e.g. your_id@yahoo.com).

Create website

1 Go to **geocities.yahoo.com/gcp** to display the GeoCities control panel. If you are not signed in to Yahoo, you'll be prompted to do this first.

Hot tip

The GeoCities control panel is the center of operations, the console from which you carry out all the activities involved in creating and managing your website.

2 Click the **Create & Update** tab to get started.

3 Scroll down to the **Basic Site Building Tools** section, with links to PageBuilder and PageWizards. We'll illustrate the process using PageWizards to create the pages and make any changes needed.

Don't forget

More experienced users may prefer to use PageBuilder (see page 162). It is also possible to build web pages using tools on the computer, and then upload the files to the website server.

PageWizards

Hot tip

PageWizards is an online site building tool, with which you customize a predefined web page template, usually to create a single-page website.

---

1 Click the **Yahoo PageWizards** link (see page 155) or go to **geocities.yahoo.com/v/w**.

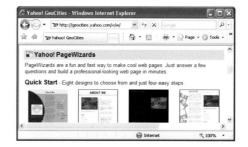

2 There's a selection of **About Me** pages in various styles, but scroll down to select the **Personal Page** as your starting point.

Hot tip

The Personal Page has an extra links section, which increases its flexibility compared to the About Me pages.

---

3 Click **Launch Yahoo PageWizards** and then click the **Begin** button.

Build your page

Before you enter the contents for the web page, choose the color scheme you prefer, then click **Next**.

Enter your name and your email address as you want them to appear on the website, then click **Next**.

Pick an image from your account, use the default image (or have no image, if desired), then click **Next**.

...cont'd

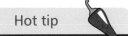

Hot tip

Click Preview at any stage, if you want to see how the page looks so far.

Don't forget

Provide Internet links that relate to your hobbies and interests, or to the main topic of your website.

③ Type in brief descriptions about yourself and about your hobbies and interests, then click **Next**.

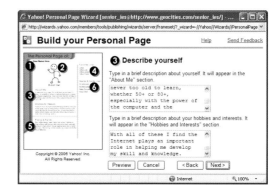

④ Provide a list of your favorite Internet links (names and addresses) such as the examples, then click **Next**.

⑤ The next section is a description of your family and friends. If you decide not to include this in your website, leave the box empty and just click **Next**.

6 The final section is for additional links. These can be used to extend the initial list, even if you didn't use the Family and Friends section. Click **Next**.

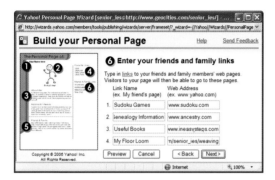

Type a name for your page. If it is the main page in your website it should be named **index**. Click **Next**.

Your web page is now complete. Make a note of the address, in this case, **www.geocities.com/senior_ies/index.html**. Note the file type .html has been added to the name you provided. Click anywhere in the table, to view the state of play at that stage.

Hot tip

This completes the six sections that were started on page 157. Note that some changes will be needed on this final section (see page 161).

Beware

You should never use capital letters, spaces or special characters in the names that you give to your pages.

159

View the web pages

Since the PageWizards tool applies changes directly at the GeoCities server, you can view your new web page without having to transfer files or wait for updating.

1 Enter the address for the web page, for example: **www.geocities.com/senior_ies/index**.

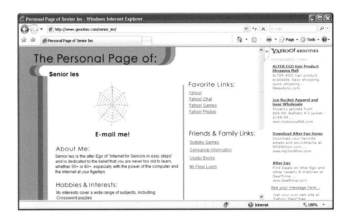

2 Create a second page for your website. In this case, we have created a web page called **weaving** which is at **www.geocities.com/senior_ies/weaving**.

3 Your home page should include a link to the new page, and it should have a home page link.

Making changes

You might decide to disguise your email address, e.g. replace **senior_ies@yahoo.com** with **senior_ies AT yahoo.com** (to thwart snooper programs searching websites for email IDs). You can make such changes using PageWizards.

1
Start the Yahoo PageWizards (see page 156) and select the appropriate type of template.

2
Select **Edit existing page**, click the down arrow and select the page by name.

3
Step through the sections, making changes as needed and clicking **Next** until you reach the final stage and click **Done** to finish.

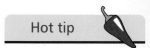

Hot tip

There are programs designed to search websites for anything that looks like an email address, to add it to mailing lists used for unsolicited emails (spam). Making your email address less obvious can help protect you from this.

Don't forget

Clicking Next at the section where you name the page (see page 159) will cause your changes to be saved to the server.

Using PageBuilder

To make more comprehensive changes to your web page, you should use the PageBuilder tool.

Hot tip

PageBuilder gives you more flexibility over your web page layout and content.

1 Click the **Yahoo PageBuilder** link (see page 155) or go to **geocities.yahoo.com/v/pb.html**.

2 Click the **Launch PageBuilder** button. You may need to disable the IE7 pop-up blocker (see page 172) while you are editing your web pages.

3 PageBuilder starts up, opening a control window and then the Java applet window itself.

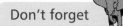

Don't forget

You must leave the control window open while you are using the PageBuilder tool.

4 Press the **Open** button and select one of your web page files, in this case **home.html**, a copy of index.html.

5 You are warned that your PageWizard file will be converted to the PageBuilder format. Click OK.

6 The web page is opened ready for editing. You can delete superfluous headings.

Beware

If you create a page in PageWizards, and then edit and save it in PageBuilder, you must no longer use PageWizards to edit that file.

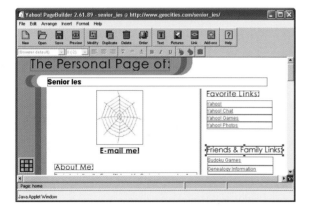

163

7 Double-click a link to change the text displayed.

8 Press the **Link** button to change the website address.

9 Press the **Save** button, to complete the changes and view the page.

Don't forget

There are many more changes you can make using PageBuilder. You can even enter html code, if you wish.

Blogs

People have always kept a daily journal. Samuel Pepys started his in 1659, and is famed for it to this day. Captain Cook kept a journal, as did many politicians. Even the fictional Adrian Mole kept a diary.

Today, everyone can do it, with the aid of the Internet and a web log, usually shortened to blog. This is a website where the entries are dated (and regularly updated) and displayed in reverse order, latest at the top. They have feedback systems, to allow readers to add their comments.

Style and taste in blogs vary enormously. To get a flavor of the range, view a variety of blogs.

1 Go to **www.bloggers.com** and click a recently updated blog in the constantly changing list.

2 Click **Next Blog** to see a randomly selected blog. Click **Back** then **Next Blog** to see another blog.

3 Type key words in the Search box, and click **Search Blogs** to find posts on particular topics.

The blogs and posts you find are different every time, but if you persevere you'll get an overview of the blog environment, and maybe stumble across something that you really enjoy.

Create a blog

If you'd like to try blogging yourself, go to the Bloggers website, scroll down and click **Create Your Blog Now**.

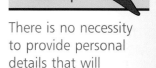

Hot tip

There is no necessity to provide personal details that will identify you. You'll find that many blogs remain anonymous.

1 Provide a user name, password, display name and email address, then click the **Continue** button.

2 Provide the title and the name for your blog, and then click **Continue**.

Don't forget

The name is part of the web address for your blog, so should be lower case letters, numbers and hyphens only. Check Availability tells you if the name is already in use.

Post to your blog

1 Choose a template and click **Continue**.

2 Your blog will be created. Click **Start Posting** to begin adding updates to it.

3 Type your post and click **Publish Post** to make the post visible at the blog site, which in our example will be **senior-ies.blogspot.com**.

RSS web feeds

Web feeds are summarizations of website changes, for example in CNN it would be new headlines. Internet Explorer toolbar has an icon for Feeds. On some websites this will be grayed and inert. Hover over it, and you are told **No feeds detected**. On other websites, the icon changes color and becomes active, and you'll be able to **View feeds**.

Hot tip

RSS stands for Really Simple Syndication, and is used to describe the technology used in creating feeds. Websites with feeds usually exhibit an XML or RSS icon.

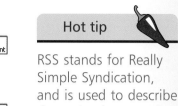

1. On **www.cnn.com**, click the down arrow next to the Feeds icon, and you'll see two CNN feeds listed.

2. Click an entry and you can view the feed, which contains frequently updated content. Click **Subscribe to this feed** to get regular updates at your computer.

> CNN.com
>
> **You are viewing a feed that contains frequently updated content.** When you subscribe to a feed, it is added to the Common Feed List. Updated information from the feed is automatically downloaded to your computer and can be viewed in Internet Explorer and other programs. Learn more about feeds.
>
> ✛ Subscribe to this feed

Hot tip

The Feeds feature is managed in the same way as your Favorites, so you can organize entries into subfolders, storing related feeds together under the same heading (see page 25).

3. Add this feed to your Feeds list in your Favorites Center.

4. You have now successfully subscribed for updates of the chosen CNN feed.

> **You've successfully subscribed to this feed!**
> Updated content can be viewed in Internet Explorer and other programs that use the Common Feed List.
>
> ☆ View my feeds

View feeds

Hot tip

The feed titles are highlighted for those feeds that have new articles available for viewing.

① To view your subscribed feeds, click **Favorites Center**, and then click the **Feeds** button.

② Select a feed from the list, to see the latest entries for that particular feed.

Hot tip

You can subscribe to feeds using Internet Explorer, and view them in other applications such as your email program.

You can leave the Feeds list visible to make it quicker to select and review all the feeds.

③ Click the **Feeds** button as above, then click the arrow icon at the top right.

④ Select individual feeds in turn from the list.

12 Internet Security

You need to take care when you visit the Internet, since it has become a target. However, there are many ways in which you can protect yourself from risk.

Browser security

IE7 (Windows XP) and IE7+ (Windows Vista) incorporate enhancements to help protect your system from attackers. The features provided include:

Your Internet browser is the primary target of malicious individuals or groups, especially identity thieves who attempt to trick you to steal your personal and financial data.

- **Phishing Filter**
  Analyses web page content and URL, and checks them against a list of questionable sites (see page 171)

- **Address Bar Protection**
  Helps block malicious sites from emulating trusted sites, by ensuring every window, pop-up or standard, shows an address bar, so you see the actual URL

- **Delete Browsing History**
  Enables you to clear cached pages, passwords, form data, cookies and history, with a single click (see page 173)

- **URL Handling Security**
  Redesigned URL parsing ensures consistent processing and minimizes possible exploits

- **Protected Mode (IE7+ only)**
  This will run the IE process with very low rights, without express user interaction on your part

- **ActiveX Opt-In**
  This reduces risk to your computer by turning off access to most ActiveX controls by default (see page 174)

- **Fix My Settings**
  The Information Bar warns you when your current security settings put your system at risk, and offers to restore the settings to the default level (see page 176)

- **Windows Defender**
  Constantly scans critical areas of the file system to ensure nothing compromises the system (see page 178)

Phishing filter

The Phishing Filter is an opt-in feature, so is only activated on request. However, Microsoft makes sure that you are aware of it, the first time you run Internet Explorer.

Hot tip

Even if you don't switch it on initially, you can always click Tools and Phishing Filter to check a site or change your settings.

① Click the box to activate the automatic checking, then click **Save Your Settings**.

② Visit any website and note the security part of the status bar as the web page loads.

③ In most cases the web page will load without hindrance. However, suspicious sites will be flagged.

Beware

Be very sure of the website, before over-riding the advice from the Phishing filter, which is updated frequently to include new threats (and correct any errors).

④ Websites that have already been reported will be blocked, and you'll be advised not to proceed.

171

Pop-up blocking

The Pop-up Blocker is turned on in Internet Explorer by default and will block most pop-ups.

1 Visit the website **www.alienskin.com**, and click on **Exposure** and then **Examples**.

2 When you click one of the pictures, you get an Information bar message saying **Pop-up blocked**.

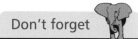
3 Click the Information bar and choose to temporarily allow pop-ups at this site (for the current visit only).

4 Choose to always allow pop-ups from this site, to have them appear on future visits.

5 If the Information Bar isn't displayed, click Tools, Pop-up Blocker then select one of the listed options.

172

Delete browsing history

As you browse the web, Internet Explorer stores details of the websites you visit and data that you type into web forms. The information Internet Explorer stores includes:

- Temporary Internet files
- Cookies
- History of your website visits
- Saved Passwords
- Temporary information

Storing this information is intended to improve your web browsing speed, but you may want to delete the recorded details if you're cleaning up your computer, or if you have been using a public computer.

To delete all of the browsing history:

1   Click Tools, and then click Delete Browsing History.

2   Click **Delete all**, and then click **Yes**.

3   Close Internet Explorer when you've finished, to clear cookies that are still in memory.

Hot tip

You can delete a specific category by clicking the associated individual Delete button.

173

Don't forget

Deleting all of the browsing history will not delete your list of favorites or your subscribed feeds.

Add-ons

Internet Explorer asks permission before running an add-on for the first time.

Hot tip

Add-ons are small applications that extend the browser (e.g. extra toolbars, animated mouse pointers, stock tickers). Often they come from websites you visit.

174

1 The first time you visit **office.microsoft.com**, the Information bar may tell you that this website wants to run the add-on **iauthzax.dll** from Microsoft.

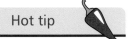

Hot tip

Internet Explorer has a list of pre-approved add-ons that have been checked and digitally signed. These are run without displaying the permissions dialog. They may come from Microsoft, your computer supplier or your ISP.

2 If you trust the website that you are visiting, then click the bar, and select **Run ActiveX Control**.

3 Click **Run** when the security warning appears.

If you believe that a new add-on is causing problems on
your system, for example causing Internet Explorer to shut
down unexpectedly, you can disable it.

1 Click Tools, Manage Add-ons, and then click Enable
or Disable Add-ons.

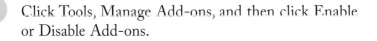

2 In the Show list, click the entry to show add-ons
that have been used by Internet Explorer.

3 Select the add-on you want to disable, and then click
the **Disable** button. Click OK to finish.

4 To reinstate a disabled add-
on, select it as above, then
click the **Enable** button, and
then click OK.

Fix My Settings

You can make changes to your Internet settings that result in your system becoming insecure.

1   Click Tools, Internet Options and the Security tab, and click Custom Level. Select an option that is labeled as not secure.

2   Click OK then Yes to change the setting.

3   Internet Explorer will now display an Information bar warning, and a message in place of your home page.

4   Click the Information Bar and select **Fix Settings for Me**.

5   Click the **Fix Settings** button to confirm, and your settings will be restored to the defaults.

Windows Update

1 Click Start, All Programs, Windows Update, or go to website **www.microsoft.com/windowsupdate**.

Hot tip

Windows Update provides you with online updates to keep your computer up-to-date with the latest security fixes.

2 Click the **Express Install** button to see what updates are available for your system.

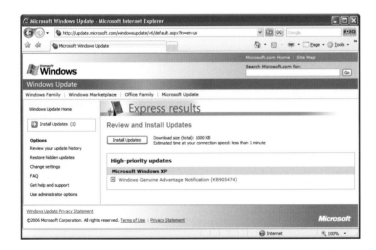

Don't forget

Upgrade to the Microsoft Update service, to receive updates for Office as well as for Windows.

3 Windows Update checks for available updates for your computer, to match your particular copy of Windows XP or Windows Vista.

Firewall and antivirus

1 Select Start, Control Panel, and then click Security Center.

2 Both Firewall and Virus protection should be On.

3 Automatic Updates should also be On, if your system is connected via DSL or Cable.

Windows XP and Windows Vista include built-in Firewall software. There are also third-party Firewall applications you can purchase and install. There's no Antivirus software included in Windows, but Microsoft does provide Windows Defender (search at **www.microsoft.com/downloads**), to protect against spyware.

You can download the AVG Free Edition antivirus software from **www.grisoft.com** for personal use, or software from other suppliers including Symantec, Sophos and McAfee.

Website Directory

These are websites from across the world that are of particular interest to seniors, to help you continue your exploration of the Internet.

50 plus information

AARP
www.aarp.org

Originally the American Association of Retired Persons, AARP is a nonprofit, nonpartisan membership organization for people aged 50 and over, whether retired or not. Note that U.S. citizenship is not a requirement for membership.

CARP
www.carp.ca

This is the Canada's association for fifty-plus, and it aims to promote the rights and quality of life of mature Canadians. See also the affiliate website **en.50plus.com**.

Hot tip

You'll find that most countries have websites for retired persons or for the over 50s. Search using your local Google to find website addresses.

Hot tip

The websites are mainly related US states and Canadian provinces, plus some international listings.

Friendly4Seniors
www.friendly4seniors.com

An excellent resource, with over 2000 websites that are reviewed and approved as senior related prior to listing. You can search for sites by category, state or keywords.

Silver Surfers
www.silversurfers.net

This was created for the UK, but does have an international flavor. It is an interface to some of the best websites for the over 50s, with links to over 10,000 – British and worldwide.

Communicating

Classmates Online   www.classmates.com

Classmates Online connects members throughout the US and Canada with friends and acquaintances from school, work and the military. Its Classmates International subsidiary operates in Sweden and in Germany.

Friends Reunited   www.friendsreunited.com

If you went to school or college in the UK, the far East or Australasia, you may be able to locate some of your old classmates by registering at the Friends Reunited website for the appropriate country.

People Search   www.whowhere.com

If you want to track down an acquaintance, not necessarily an old school or army mate, this website will help you find updated phone numbers and address information, find email addresses and contact information, or find a name and address using a phone number.

181

Hot tip

When you look back and realize how many people you have lost touch with over the years, perhaps you'll feel the urge to find out where they are now, and what has happened to them.

Hot tip

The Lycos WhoWhere people search is just one of the many directory based websites that allow you to search for people (and businesses).

Digital photography

Links to satellite images are provided for photographs in areas covered by the Google map service.

Satellite view

Photographic Walks   www.all-free-photos.com

A collection of over 900 high resolution images of European walks and travels, panoramic views included, in galleries of castles and parks, towns and villages, landscapes etc.

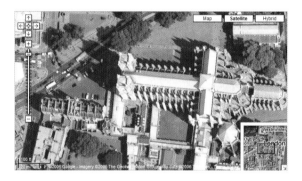

Satellite Views   maps.google.com

At the Google Maps site, search for a location, for example the House of Commons in London, UK. Then click the Satellite button to view from above, zooming in to reveal as much detail as the available satellite photographs allow.

Tips   www.internetbrothers.com/phototips.htm

Visit the PhotoTips page at the Internet Brothers website for a selection of digital photography tips and tutorials. For example, there is a step-by-step guide on how to take a series of overlapping digital photos and turn them into a 360° panorama video.

You will need software such as Apple's QTVR Authoring Studio to stitch the photos together into a QuickTime video.

182

Learning

Elderhostel   www.elderhostel.org

Elderhostel is a not-for-profit educational travel organization providing short, on-campus courses for people 55 and over, with 8,000 offerings a year in more than 90 countries.

SeniorNet   www.seniornet.org

SeniorNet is aimed at computer-using adults, age 50 and older. It supports over 240 Learning Centers throughout the U.S. and in other countries, publishes

newsletters and instructional materials, and supports online round table discussions at the website.

U3A   www.harrowu3a.co.uk/u3a_sites.html

U3A (University of the Third Age) is an international organization whose aims are the education and stimulation of retired members of the community. The Harrow U3A maintains a list by country of links to U3A and other institutes for learning in retirement.

Publishing on the Internet

Hot tip

In this particular website, the case of the web page address does not matter. If you enter the address as all lowercase it will be adjusted to partial capitalization.

Accessibility Initiative www.w3.org/wai/references/quicktips/overview.php

Seniors know better than most, how web pages can become unreadable due to poor color, contrast, etc. This overview summarizes the key concepts of accessible web design (e.g. a site suitable for the visually impaired) as a set of quick tips.

Piers Anthony www.hipiers.com/publishing.html

Piers Anthony (the writer of the Xanth fantasy series) and his blog-style survey of Internet publishers may be useful, when you finish that novel you've always meant to write.

Hot tip

The website address changes to the current year, for example, 2006.bloggies.com. You can also visit the results for previous years, for example, 2005.bloggies.com.

Weblog Awards www.bloggies.com

This website tells you how to nominate weblogs for the various categories, gives details of the judging procedure and lists the finalists and the winning entry for each category.

Reference material

GWR   www.guinnessworldrecords.com

Whenever you wonder what's the largest (or any other -est), you'll find the answer at the Guinness World Records site.

Merck Manual   www.merck.com/pubs

Merck makes available a series of online manuals, including the Merck Manual of Medical Information – Home Edition which translates complex medical information into plain language. There's also an online Merck Manual of Health & Aging.

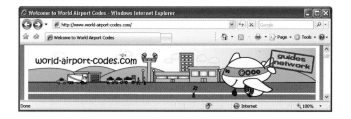

Maporama   www.maporama.com

Maporama is the most wide ranging mapping service, with maps for over 200 countries, and directions to and within over 60 countries including the United States, Canada, Europe, Asia and Australia. It generates routes with up to 3 stopovers, and you can specify road preferences.

World Airport Codes   world-airport-codes.com

With almost 10,000 listed, this site provides airport codes, abbreviations, runway lengths, location maps and other information for almost every airport in the world.

Hot tip

As this example shows, it isn't always necessary to enter the full website address. Here we omit www. but the browser still finds the website.

Travel

50plus Expeditions   www.50plusexpeditions.com

Adventure trips designed and selected specifically for active travelers 50 and over, who enjoy activities such as wilderness trips, rafting on a jungle river or riding an elephant.

French Waterways   www.frenchwaterways.net

A different way to visit and explore France, and discover many of its hidden treasures. You will also experience gourmet cuisine, fine wine and unique sightseeing excursions to ancient villages, castles, cafes and markets.

OAG (official airline guide)   www.oag.com

OAG is a global travel and transport information company, with airline, airport, country and city guides, plus full details of loyalty card schemes (click the **Frequent Flyer** link).

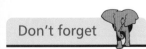

Don't forget

Saga also market insurance and finance products, there's a Saga Magazine and there are Saga radio stations, all aimed at the 50+ audience.

Saga Holidays   www.saga.co.uk/travel

The Saga Group focuses exclusively on the provision of services for people 50 and over. These include holidays to worldwide destinations, from cruises to self-catering.

Index

H

I

J

Q

R

S

T